CW01044457

François Bodet

Breguet, the story of a passion 1973-1987

As told to Françoise Favre

ISBN 978-2-940506-10-1

Publishing Managers: Fabrice Mugnier and Suzanne Wettstein

English Translation: Susan Jacquet, Transcribe

Printing: IRL plus SA, Renens, Switzerland
Printed and bound in Switzerland

printed in
switzerland

See our publications on watches and jewellery on our website:
www.watchprint.com

I dedicate this book

… to my grandfather Paul Bodet (October 8th 1878 to November 9th 1935), a watchmaker in Angers, of whom I cherish fond thoughts across the ages;

to my wife Marie-Laure;

to my children Marina, Alexia and Jean-Eric;

and to my grandchildren, Timéo, Nino, Lilia, Milia, Eliot and others still to come.

PUBLISHER'S NOTE

This book is written as a type of intimate journal, which combines childhood memories with those of a young appprentice and all the experiences gained and born of encounters – firstly with the great names in jewellery and subsequently in watchmaking. It is above all a testimony and recounts the birth of a passion dedicated to an emblematic figure in watch-making: Breguet.

Mr François Bodet, today aged 72, has allowed his thoughts to flow freely to help us grasp, through his own story, the profound significance of time in the evolution of knowledge.

As well as devoting his life to highlighting and magnifying the pocket watches of yesteryear while safeguarding their essence, he succeeded in promoting Breguet internationally.

These pages are filled with a sense of humility nurtured by a conviction that – as the author aptly expresses it – knowledge is passed on by individuals serving as guiding lights in fostering the growth of talent.

All his masters are named and due tribute is paid to them, since it is so clearly true that the current renown of Breguet stems from the combined talents of all those who made it possible to perceive "the nostalgic sound of the soul" in each of these watches.

FOREWORD

It was back in 1983 that I first heard the news that Mr François Bodet, supported by a small team of watchmakers with "golden hands", had renewed production of timepieces worthy of Abraham-Louis Breguet's exceptional heritage. Without the slightest hesitation, I decided to visit him at his workshops in the beautiful Vallée de Joux.

During our first meeting, Mr Bodet was somewhat surprised at my interest in becoming a dealer for the brand in my capacity as a retailer in a tourist resort. It must be mentioned that he was not particularly familiar with my name, nor indeed with the town of Interlaken. By talking as one watchmaker to another about Abraham-Louis Breguet's achievements and inventions, I think Mr Bodet quickly sensed my passion for the brand. My keen desire to become part of an adventure involving the reconstruction of a great name from the past and a brand with an incredible history was infectious. The contact was made and the business up and running!

Mr Bodet is a genius with boundless passion. He has succeeded in recreating watches like the pocket watches of the past while retaining their inspiration and their essence.

All the foundations of Breguet's incredible success today were put in place during this exceptional re-launch, which was the result of the unconditional love of a single man, François Bodet.

I would like to wish the readers of this book immense pleasure in discovering all the effort, passion and hard work it took to achieve this human adventure.

Congratulations on this huge, amazing endeavour!

Jürg Kirchhofer
Kirchhofer, Interlaken

CONTENTS

CHAPTER 1

EXPLORING THE MYSTERIES OF WATCHMAKING

The Bodet-Pasquier jeweller's in Angers enjoyed a sterling reputation and was known far and wide. At the helm was my father, who also guided my first professional steps when he took me on as an apprentice after I completed my schooling that had done little to arouse my interest.

He was a figure of authority both at work and at home. He doubtless had little choice, since being the father of a family of ten children probably requires a degree of discipline. Paul Bodet excelled in selling jewellery, for which he not only had the right personality, but also a refined, aristocratic bearing and a good measure of insight. He had initially planned to study medicine, but circumstances forced him to take over his father's business.

Born on November 21st 1942, I was the family's sixth child. As soon as I reached school age, I was sent to the *Frères à Quatre bras* Catholic school in Nantes, which meant getting up at 5am on Monday mornings and walking to the train station alone, in the cold and dark.

My masters were no less authoritarian and strict than the paternal rule I had already experienced at home, and I felt it all the more acutely in that I was a boarder.

My young life was subjected to this discipline from which there was no escape! I still remember the punishment that was meted out to me by a priest, one of my teachers, for having teased a schoolmate: a story by La Fontaine to learn by heart and recite every evening for a month. At the end of my recital I was systematically given a slap on both sides of my head that momentarily deafened me…

I still vividly recall those summer holidays when, for a month and a half, my parents sent me to a priest in Sarthe so that he could help me with my maths! Here too, I was on the receiving end of slaps throughout my stay. I lived with a number of countesses in a little chateau where rats nibbled on my soap and towel in my room…

Affection and gentleness had no place in the landscape of my childhood and even if, from a human perspective, this must have had some effect, my mind learned to take the blows unflinchingly, thus keeping both emotion and adversity at bay… This proved an essential lesson to which I was to refer throughout my life. As far as the rest is concerned, any sensitivity and affection were to remain repressed in my inner self and difficult to express.

From my mother, Paulette Bodet, a pianist and painter, I inherited my sense of both beauty and art in ample measure. She ran the shop, while keeping an eye on her large family and looking after the household. A strong woman, who never complained, she instilled in me the same spirit that she herself radiated.

Being an apprentice was not a particularly welcome choice, but my father saw in me a son to take over from him as the head of the family business. In order to do this, I needed a watchmaker-jeweller diploma, so my career path was apparently cast in stone…

My grandfather and I in 1953.
I was 11 years old.

Wearing grey overalls, just like all the other apprentices, I heard my father tell the clients "I only have one child who has succeeded and that is the one with the baccalaureate…" He wasn't referring to me and that single sentence inflicted pain that I endured in silence. He used to send me to take parcels to the station with a hand-drawn cart – into which travellers who saw me and thought I was a porter used to put their suitcases!

I studied watchmaking in my father's workshop under the responsibility of one of the finest French craftsmen (*Meilleur Ouvrier de France*). It was a good education! Bent intently over the mechanisms of a watch, I not only learned to look, but to see: in just a few minutes, with my eye glued to the magnifying glass, it was essential to be capable of

The Bodet-Pasquier boutique, on Boulevard Foch in Angers, Maine et Loire, France, 1954.

detecting any faults or flaws in its running. My eye was to become my most efficient tool. Little by little, it became sharper and the tiniest details remained imprinted on my mind, enabling me to make swift, spontaneous assessments.

These four years of watchmaking training were invaluable to me. I first learned to make my tools by hand, starting with my screwdrivers from start to finish, prior to taking on clocks and alarm clocks soon after, and then pocket watches with a 24''' and 19''' diameter (in watchmaker's jargon, the symbol ''' stands for a *ligne* = 2.25 mm). As was expected of me, I gradually became capable of working on smaller and smaller models. I also learned how to repair a watch completely. While there are so many different aspects in the elements composing a timepiece that four years is not enough to learn them all, my training included an apprenticeship as a pivot-maker. Starting with pocket watch staffs, I "burnished" ever smaller pivots, right the way down to those required for 12''' pocket watches! In the beginning, I took hours to finish my pivots and very often broke them after endless work and patience! Hence my subsequent interest in Daniel Roth who pivoted incredibly tiny arbors at Audemars Piguet, displaying truly amazing workmanship.

Little by little, I acquired certain points of reference that would prove extremely useful in my future professional endeavours. Especially since my apprenticeship offered fine opportunities to expand my knowledge. One of my father's suppliers, Georges Schmaus, a diamond dealer, had secretly guessed my flair for jewellery and offered to take me to his Parisian offices in order to train me in precious stones. I spent several months with him. He was a well-known character in the jewellery profession and he had an incredible stock of stones. I learnt to analyse, measure and rate the quality of stones and their colours.

During the first few days of my internship, he asked me to empty the dustbin. I did so. Emptying a diamond dealer's dustbin means sorting out the contents prior to throwing them away… and amongst the trash I found a ruby. I gave it back to my apprenticeship master, who was very pleased… If it was a test of my honesty, I passed it with flying colours!

Whenever he went out, he took me with him. We went to the gem-setter or the polisher, we strolled along the Rue Richelieu… When we reached the foot of a building, he would whistle and upon hearing this signal, the gem-setter would stick his head out of a dormer window on the fifth floor, cast a glance to check who was there, and then come down to fetch the precious stones which needed polishing and setting. This memory lingers like the symbol of another era, albeit not so long ago, when doing and making objects – including the most precious – involved exchanges from hand-to-hand exchanges, person-to-person communication and relatively simple procedures.

In addition to providing such breadth and depth of instruction, this remarkable man encouraged me to take a course in natural pearls, with Jacques Biennenfeld, a great master in this field based in the Rue Lafayette. This represented an extremely rare training opportunity.

Once again, over a period of several months, I learned to string natural pearls into a necklace using cannetille, the precious gold or silver thread used to sew in the clasp – and to appraise them in the northern light that enhanced the true colours of the pearls.

I took all this knowledge on board with great passion. The future would confirm how fortunate I had been with these people and their teaching and I felt an enormous sense of gratitude. Those years of watchmaking training in my father's workshop were also to play a key role because, when the time came, I was able to understand watchmakers and their concerns and meet their expectations…

From a very early age, I suffered from a handicap: stuttering. I was unable to say "a" and "o", which made "Hallo" an impossible word. When I was an apprentice at my father's workshop, I was petrified of the telephone.

I resolved this handicap in my own way. From 1963-1964, I did my military service in a very tough battalion called the Blue Berets. This did not prevent me from climbing the ranks. By force of circumstance, I had to say: "On my command…" Impossible.

I was incapable of saying this sentence and because I couldn't say it, I was imprisoned for refusing to give orders. So clearly, I needed to get over this handicap, but how?

I thought of offering to volunteer for the *semaine* (week-long command), which meant managing a battalion between the officers and several hundred people and involved issuing a constant stream of commands. "I'm going to yell!" I thought… I was the perfect commander, since it was all about shouting! The more I yelled, the less I stuttered.

I had found the solution! Instead of taking my turn to assume the *semaine* once, as is generally the case, I volunteered seven or eight times! That became my treatment: in order to stop stuttering, I had to be in charge for the week!

During my military service, I used my free time to repair watches. I did things that were generally done at a workbench on the hut's coal-fired stove. I heated the shellac, a special product used to stabilise the ruby pallet stones of the watch's lever escapement and I got the timepieces beating again and the hands running.

My four-year apprenticeship spent at my father's workshop was already serving its purpose! It enabled me to earn a bit of money with which I bought a Citroen 4 CV, so that my feeling of independence could actually become more of a reality!

With my military service complete and my certificate of professional aptitude in my pocket, I took courses in 1965-66 at the *Ecole du Louvre* in the painting department and subsequently at the *Ecole de Dessins de Bijoux* (jewellery design school) in Paris.

When it came to jewellery, I wanted to try anything that came my way. Twice a week, at the Hôtel Drouot auctions, I was allowed to try my skill at appraising the pieces that were to be sold. Once again, I learnt to observe, detail, reposition the object in its historical context, and to assess the value of items.

I had no desire to stop there. The passion for learning had me in its grip in the same way that I was fired by a passion for jewellery. I decided to enrol at the Gemological Institute in London.

I spent so much time in the Gemmology section of the Natural History Museum that I even had my own stool! Two rich years of study lay ahead of me (1967-1968), but I needed to find a means of paying my way. I found a few hours of housework that I didn't turn down, and which included polishing the silver and waxing the furniture. Why not? The owner of the home in question was a colonel in the Queen's Guard. It didn't take long for an idea nurtured by my passion for jewellery to form in my head: what were the chances of my being introduced and given a chance to look at the Queen's jewellery? I was so taken with the idea that it actually happened: Garrard, one of the great London jewellers, allowed me to look at certain jewels and other pieces!

And since I was in London, why not take advantage of the experience of a two or three-month internship in Omega's After-Sales Service at Saffron Hill? So that's exactly what I did!

After my stay in London, an Iranian friend who was studying at the cinema school in Paris invited me to accompany him on a two-month trip to Iran. He was going to give presentations on filmmaking, in which I also played a role by talking about philosophical themes in films.

My real aim was naturally to see the Shah's jewellery… One day, my wish was granted. I was led down to the basement of an American bank and introduced to the Shah's enormous safes! Incredible jewellery, gigantic globes made of diamonds with sapphire oceans, Van Cleef diadems. I experienced some truly fabulous moments amid a legendary world. Surrounded by bodyguards who left me to my own devices, I spent two or three days contemplating these fascinating beauties, cleaning a few pieces and giving assorted advice.

I was lucky enough to sit on the Shah's throne, entirely set with "pigeon's blood" rubies! It was incredible! I was at the very heart of my passion! Like a guiding thread, this led me towards everything that would help to fulfil and intensify my experience, as well as teaching me more and more… I never went anywhere without visiting a museum and little by little an unusual, out of the ordinary education took shape, which not only lived within me, but actually became part of me.

Many wonders and surprises punctuated my discoveries on the streets of Iran: churches with domes sparkling with gold and fascinating characters… I still remember the evenings spent in the company of a magnificent stringed instrument maker whose hands gave birth to violins, including those belonging to Paul and David Oïstrakh. Raised with the very soul of these instruments, his daughter was the first violin in the Tehran Orchestra.

At Tabriz, we were invited to visit the prosecutor's office. Upon entering, we were surprised to see five people sitting on the floor on either side of the door, with balls and chains on their ankles. They were awaiting their sentences! A chilling image that one would only expect to see in days gone by or in historical films. Not everything in human life is made of gold and precious stones…

Other far-off places such as the United States beckoned me. I yearned for the freedom afforded by this land and the possibility of earning a little money. I set off for an eight-month stay during which I worked in restaurants in Atlanta, initially as a cleaner and a month later, as head of the cleaners. Two months on, by dint of hard work, I was put in charge of the restaurant night shift!

A jeweller client from Atlanta often came to the restaurant. He wore a signet ring on his finger with a closed-set ruby. We had often chatted together and he was aware of my passion for precious stones. In order to test my skill, he asked me how much the stone on his signet ring weighed. With a closed setting it is hard to tell, so I took a guess: "1.05 carats". It actually weighed 1.03 carats and he was so impressed that he wanted to hire me on the spot!

I was young and slightly tempted by the offer, but in the end did not take him up on it. I was not interested in a future in the United States where jewellery did not enjoy the same prestige as in Europe… I earned a good living at the restaurant and was just a visitor in the country, who would soon be returning to France.

It was time to give my career a go in the true sense of the term. Grenoble was the first stop from 1968 to 1970, at Gay Jewellers, who were known to my father. The House of Jacques Gay didn't usually take interns but despite this, they agreed to let me come and further my training with them. Along with sales, I learned the commercial side of the trade. I was in charge of the precious stones portfolio, a responsibility that was a logical result of the knowledge acquired to date.

"Jacques Gay" was a large company. It employed some 20 people between the watchmaking and jewellery workshops and the shop itself, and encompassed the full spectrum of skills involved in the business. Sales were substantial in every sector: jewellery, watchmaking, crystal and silverware. It was undoubtedly an important internship and one which, along with enabling me to exercise my abilities in various domains, also had an impact on my private life.

It was there in Grenoble that I met the woman who was to become my wife! Lively, happy, thoughtful and deeply generous, Marie-Laure would in fact be far more than a wife. The following pages will tell the tale of all the twists and turns in my life. She made both my passion and my worries her own, bringing me the strength I desperately needed along with a healthy dose of intelligence!

1971-1972 brought a stint at Pellegrin jeweller's in Marseille. A specialist in the production of luxury jewellery and precious stone appraisals, it was the biggest jeweller's in the French provinces and worthy of the Place Vendôme from every point of view.

The atmosphere in the shop exuded elegance. Everything was focused on design, stones, expertise and production. For me it was a wonderful opportunity to spend nearly two years in this jewellery temple.

The first saleswoman who witnessed the arrival of this youngster reacted with great caution… She waited for the second day before asking me the price of a natural pearl necklace and was amazed to hear me tell her the correct price! The test had thus been taken and passed! My experience at Biennenfeld on Rue Lafayette in Paris had paid off!

I was not amongst those who feel the need to boast. Apart from the people who hired me, I never talked about my career, what I had learned or what I had been trained to do. It was only little by little that the people with whom I worked directly got to know me.

Georges Pellegrin and Jean-François, his son, with whom I shared the same office, were skilled when it came to procurement as well as brilliantly creative. From the very moment when they would buy precious stones, they knew exactly what they were going to make with them. It was fantastic and they displayed an unparalleled knowledge of the trade.

I sat next to Jean-François and our job was to produce, to sell, to appraise jewellery and to take care of the gemstone portfolio. When Mr Pellegrin was asked for an appraisal, he took out his stopwatch. Our study was not allowed to take longer than the minute we were allocated, so there was no place for hesitation! The question was all about whether you had an eye or you didn't. Taking your time would change nothing with regard to the estimate! We had to know the cost price, the cost of setting and the cost of the stones of every ring, every necklace! What an apprenticeship and what an experience!

I reached the point of being able to distinguish a dozen different shades of white in diamonds. Both at Pellegrin and Gay, my eye selected one of those whites. When the diamond dealers came, this internal colour chart never let me down. It also helped when it came to observing natural pearls with all those incredibly subtle tones that were so familiar to me! However, this sharpness needed to be exercised all the time: as soon as I used it a bit less, my eye lost something of its ability and it took some time to readjust in order to once again be spot on with the shades.

Practice and experience were exactly what I needed to improve my armoury. Those years of jewellery at Pellegrin were one of the highlights of my entire career.

Foreground: Gold hand-worked "Lépine".
Background : *Tact* watch with
gold hand-worked case.

CHAPTER 2

THE HOUSE OF CHAUMET

At the end of 1972, through the intermediary of Mr Charles Lefèvre, a director at Vacheron Constantin, a prestigious door was to open for me at the House of Chaumet on Place Vendôme.

Mr Lefèvre had talked about me and I was asked to show up for a number of tests. The results revealed that I had a stubborn nature and I was duly hired by the renowned jewellery company, founded in 1780.

Here too, apart from the bosses, nobody knew what I had done previously. I was given an office next to the prestigious Louis XVI salon. The setting was strikingly beautiful, since this salon was the oldest in the Place Vendôme and was created by Bélanger for the Lord of Saint James, the General Treasurer of the navy of King Louis XVI. On the wall, painted by Robert Lefèvre, was a portrait of Marie-Louise, the Empress of France, wearing a necklace made by Chaumet as a gift to commemorate the birth of the King of Rome.

It was in this salon that Fréderic Chopin played and composed during the last four months of his life and in which he died on October 17th 1849, at a time when the stately townhouse was home to the Russian Embassy in Paris.

The parquet flooring is entirely made of ebony and rosewood marquetry with a wind rose positioned exactly in the centre. Anyone entering this place cannot fail to be impressed with the elegance before him.

When I joined it, the House of Chaumet was first and foremost the realm of two brothers, Jacques and Pierre Chaumet. Both were endowed with keen intelligence, mastery of their profession, analytical skills, finely developed expertise and elegance… A complete state of mind. It was a world of finely cut suits, waistcoats, silk pocket handkerchiefs, kissing a lady's hand… It was not a world based on appearance, but rather one that expressed its culture and philosophy through appearances. There were nine deliverymen, all in livery. When I drafted a letter, which was naturally handwritten, I rang for the head attendant who sent a deliveryman. I left the letter on a silver tray, and it would return to me on a silver tray, duly typed, three or four hours later. A very different sphere from our industrialised, digital world.

Throughout 1973, I had no clearly defined activity. Then it was agreed that I would create a shop called "Les Temporelles Chaumet", in which watches and jewellery-watches would be displayed and sold. Leaving jewellery behind for watches was a difficult time, but

The House of Chaumet
on Place Vendôme, Paris.

25

I had to get over my disappointment… Working on the Place Vendôme requires a number of diplomatic virtues…

All was not completely lost, because I was nevertheless able to create a set of small jewellery items for Japan!

The Chaumet Salons,
Place Vendôme, Paris

I was going to approach Breguet from the perspective of a jeweller!

I often heard one little sentence spoken by experienced salespeople: "A watch that is sold is a lost client!" This preconceived idea had to be erased to the point where it was no longer remotely true!

The young man that I was understood that I needed to get on with the job – which required flexibility, firmness, clear perspectives, moving forward with caution while taking as many people as possible along, knowing how to remain modest, revealing nothing while constantly taking up challenges!

The boutique named "Les Temporelles Chaumet", of which I was the manager, represented the Audemars Piguet, Chopard, Corum, Delaneau, Ebel, Genta (Geneva), Jaeger-LeCoultre and Rolex brands, which taught me a lot about the world of watchmaking because we were one of their first representatives in France. I was able to visit all their factories. Seven hundred pieces sold a year was an indication of the success enjoyed by "Les Temporelles Chaumet".

In 1970, Jacques and Pierre Chaumet had acquired Breguet for a modest sum, with no exact aim in mind. They expressed a desire for me to step in. In 1975, two years after the creation of "'Les Temporelles Chaumet", they entrusted the responsibility of Breguet to me in order to do something with this great name.

Real jewellers do not make watches. These are two different sectors and mindsets that are largely ignorant of each other, as well as two completely independent skill sets. Jewellery. Watchmaking. The timeless on the one hand and the temporal on the other, with no real bridge between the two. I was therefore going to approach Breguet from the perspective of a jeweller!

The future of my parents' jewellery business was entrusted to my brother, Michel Bodet, who was a jeweller to his very soul and a great connoisseur of precious stones. His creations demonstrated an enormous sense of artistry. It is rare for someone to be both designer and diamond dealer! These criteria endowed the Bodet jeweller's store with the ultimate touch of class and contributed to its success with its clientele.

Abraham-Louis Breguet,
born 1747 in Neuchâtel.
Died 1823.

CHAPTER 3

THE HOUSE OF BREGUET

B reguet… a name that resounds like a legend, a dream and a history… the awakening of a sleeping beauty.

Let us travel back across the centuries and across Europe to meet Abraham-Louis Breguet. During the troubled times of the revocation of the Edict of Nantes, Abraham-Louis' parents had fled Picardy to seek asylum in Switzerland. It was there, in the town of Neuchâtel, that Abraham-Louis was born in 1747. A brilliant destiny awaited him, of which he was to be the ingenious architect…

At barely 15 years of age, he found himself at Versailles, where his step-father wanted him to learn the watchmaking trade, recognised as an art at the time.

Versailles. A whole new world! Abraham-Louis attended the Collège Mazarin where he studied physics and mathematics, both of which he found intensely fascinating. He had a lively passion and an even livelier intelligence; everyone recognised he was a brilliant student.

Having attracted the attention of Louis XV, Abraham-Louis moved to the Quai de l'Horloge in Paris. The winds of love had made their presence felt and at 20, he married Marie-Louise Lhuillier. Both aware of and confident in his talent, his in-laws provided financial support and Abraham-Louis established his own workshop on the Quai de l'Horloge. This was a fitting setting for his genius and it was there that he made the first "perfect" automatic watch that could run for eight years without a single service and without losing time!

His reputation had reached the salons of Versailles and the courts of England, Russia and Prussia. But storm clouds were gathering in the skies of French history. In 1789, the crowds marched on the Bastille… Marie-Antoinette, the Duke of Orléans and Frederick II of Prussia had all assured Abraham-Louis Breguet of their loyalty, but his connections with the nobility were known to all and in 1793, under threat during the dark days of the Reign of Terror, Breguet was forced into exile in his native country – which was of course Switzerland!

Determined to continue his magnificent adventure, he opened a workshop in Le Locle, hired a number of watchmakers and continued to deliver timepieces to the courts of England and Russia.

Abraham-Louis was a man who liked a challenge, and stopping after his initial success made no sense to his highly inventive mind. Using calculations to do research, he designed the perpetual calendar, the tourbillon – an ingenious mechanism that compensates for the varying rates of the balance wheel due to the effects of gravity – the ruby cylinder, the *sympathique* clock, the constant-force escapement, the *tact* watch, and the anti-shock device, tested by Abraham-Louis Breguet himself under the astonished gaze of Talleyrand!

Certain people, envious of his success, took advantage of his exile to copy him. Fakes abounded which the perpetrators were brazen enough to sell for high prices. When he became aware of this, Abraham-Louis signed his creations with a secret signature that was almost invisible to the naked eye, drawn with the very fine point of a pantograph and rendering any imitation impossible!

After two years of violence and blood-letting, Abraham-Louis returned to Paris to find his workshop ransacked and his belongings destroyed. Without losing heart, he managed to obtain considerable compensation from the youthful Republic, which enabled him to start over again with the same degree of passion and genius as before.

The most important figures of the time clamoured for a piece of his talent, including Queen Victoria, Louis XVII, Baron Hottinguer, the Duke de Morny, Pushkin and Stendhal, Alexander Dumas and Jules Verne. Literature also proved the gateway to becoming a legend and Phileas Fogg, the hero of Jules Verne, was able to complete his trip around the world in 80 days thanks to a Breguet chronometer!

While Breguet's success was first and foremost due to his inherent genius, there is no doubt that it was bolstered by another of his talents: his idea of a workshop in which watchmakers and specialists pooled their skills. He won a number of awards including a gold medal at the *Exposition des Industries Françaises* (Exhibition of French Industry) in 1798 and again in 1819. He was also appointed official supplier to the Ministry of the Navy and dubbed a Knight of the Legion of Honour in 1819.

When he died on September 17th 1823, Breguet's name and prestige echoed far and wide. This reputation was upheld by Louis-Antoine Breguet, who joined the company in 1807, and subsequently by his son, Louis-François, who took over in 1833. The brand enjoyed a new boom by embracing progress and modernity with the arrival on the market of the first electric clocks.

Louis-François Breguet was a renowned scientist who researched avenues different from those investigated by his grandfather, but also with great success. However, despite his many inventions, he was unable to devote himself to every form of science, and in 1867 relinquished control of the watchmaking workshop and the Breguet signature to his workshop foreman, Edward Brown.

Generations of Browns succeeded each other, continuing production under the Breguet names and cultivating associations with other great names such as de La Rochefoucauld, de Rothschild, Guerlain, the Prince of Broglia and many other illustrious figures.

In 1970, Breguet came under the aegis of the House of Chaumet and I found myself with a daunting task ahead of me. There were only two or three old watches in stock along with the archive documents – historical books in which all the names of famous Breguet clients throughout history were recorded. As a result, there was nothing substantial with which to start work!

Messrs Renoud and Gastelier, watchmakers established on the Rue de la Paix in Paris, took care of old Breguet pieces and repaired models belonging to the brand, providing few clues liable to point me in the right direction. It was really hard to work out what style I was going to impart to Breguet. Finding myself at a dead-end, I decided to approach important Breguet collectors as well as a number of museum curators in Switzerland, notably Mr André Curtit, curator of the *Musée International d'Horlogerie* in La Chaux-de-Fonds.

Through the intermediary of the brands that I represented, a profile gradually began to emerge and little by little, a number of pieces began popping up in Paris, with Mr Gastelier. For the first watches I made, I used Manufacture movements. The Place Vendôme address was an open sesame that worked wonders with the manufacturers!

In 1973 and 1974, "moon phases" were all the rage, as were skeletonised watches. I had a case manufacturer in Paris and I was lucky enough to have the support of Charles Lefèvre, CEO of Vacheron Constantin.

We also worked with Gérald Genta of Geneva, a watch designer who was already making some Chaumet watches (particularly the "Chaumet 12" models) and to whom we entrusted the creation of a number of Breguet pieces sold on the Place Vendôme.

The Breguet style took shape gradually, shortly before the period between 1973 and 1975 when I was still tentatively finding my way. It was made in Paris.

But the real breakthrough took place between 1975 and 1976 with Breguet's pioneering watchmakers, mainly thanks to their close collaboration with the artisans of the watch cases, dials and hands.

The historical pieces bore vibrant testimony in stylistic terms, while Breguet collectors provided highly informed input.

Lire l'heure "Breguet" chez Chaumet.

This resulted in defining the five distinctive features of a Breguet: the hand-crafted fluting on the caseband, the Breguet dial hand-engraved on a rose engine, the Breguet hand with its characteristic eccentric, hollowed 'moon' tip, the extremely distinctive buckle and the easily recognisable case lugs.

The beginnings were very modest given the tiny number of watches created. I needed to ensure that I attracted favourable feedback on what I was doing with Breguet in order to gain the confidence of my bosses. The Chaumet brothers were clear as to what they wanted: "Les Temporelles Chaumet" must make a profit and the profits would in turn be used to to finance Breguet. No "Temporelles", no Breguet.

Among those we worked with in this adventure, we came across an envious individual who sought to be taken for Breguet – proof in itself that the winds of success were beginning to blow.

Little by little, I became increasingly involved in the watchmaking policy of Chaumet, which had five boutiques across the world. That made things easier, because this role enabled me quite naturally to impose distribution of the Breguet watches that I was producing in Paris. Chaumet was a key support and the brand's exclusive representative, so I targeted jewellery rather than watchmaking clients for Breguet.

I equipped the Breguet watches made in Paris with Hermès leather straps – a strategic alliance in which the well-known prestige of this brand implicitly signified that of Breguet. Mechanical watchmaking thereby identified with Parisian luxury.

Later on in Japan, driven by this same mindset, I offered each client a bottle of Eau Impériale by Guerlain. This association of images delighted the Japanese who have always been able to recognise enduring elegance.

These associations took place all the more easily because these brands – Hermès, Guerlain, Chaumet and Breguet – all belonged to the Comité Colbert, which enjoyed unquestioned credibility. Founded in 1954, the Comité Colbert united 75 companies involved in the sharing and promotion of tradition and modernity, know-how and creation, history and innovation, both in France and on the international scene.

Around 1975, I had sold a "grande sonnerie" (grand strike) watch by subscription to a collector, for a large amount of money.

When I say "by subscription", I mean that a down payment was made well before the delivery, which is exactly how Abraham-Louis Breguet operated in his day. Given that production took several months and indeed sometimes years, this method enabled him to make a living and to pay his watchmakers.

Upon discovering the cost of this "grande sonnerie", the Chaumet were dumbstruck at the realisation of just how high the price of highly complicated watchmaking models could soar.

I was lucky enough to be able to hire exceptional salesladies who were incredibly talented and anyone who came into the shop inevitably left with a watch! As elegant and efficient agents, their contribution to the success of both "Les Temporelles Chaumet" and Breguet itself was key.

Other than the five Chaumet shops around the world, Pierre Chaumet also enjoyed considerable opportunities in Morocco where he was very close to His Majesty King Hassan II, who also took an interest in Breguet watches. This relationship was not widely known and is illustrated by an anecdote passed on to me in this regard:

One day, when Pierre Chaumet was absent, his housekeeper answered the phone …

Upon his return, he asked her: "Was everything alright?"

"Yes," she replied in a somewhat detached manner, "someone telephoned and wanted to talk to you. I asked who it was and he said: 'the King of Morocco'..."

"Oh! And what did you reply?"

"That I was the Queen of England!"

Did it require a great deal of diplomacy for Pierre Chaumet to fix this unfortunate incident? I never found out, but I don't think it can have been too hard because he was by nature a refined and elegant man.

Interest in the Breguet brand, its production and its reputation thus continued to grow.

By 1974, given the high prices for tools charged by the manufacturers with whom I dealt, it was definitely time to set about achieving greater independence.

| François Bodet

CHAPTER 4

BREGUET IN THE VALLÉE DE JOUX AND THE PIONEERING WATCHMAKERS

T he time to take a decision had come. Paris, La Chaux-de-Fonds or the Vallée de Joux: where would the best place be to manufacture Breguet watches? It swiftly became apparent that Breguet could not develop based on the culture of a bustling metropolis such as Paris. I needed skills stemming from longstanding and demanding expertise in order to guarantee a noble heritage.

Switzerland cultivated the spirit of beautiful watchmaking and was heir to ancestral traditions. In 1974, Georges Golay, the CEO of Audemars Piguet – which was represented by "Les Temporelles Chaumet" – encouraged me to come and set up here, which I did. I asked him about the possibility of partnering with a number of watchmakers who worked for his company. With his approval, I in due course hired six or seven people, until he called a halt! He came to see the Chaumet brothers at the Place Vendôme directly and told us he wanted it to stop immediately!

I had been to Audemars Piguet in Le Brassus several times previously and had met the pivot-maker who machined tiny movement arbors. My watchmaking origins with my father enabled me to appreciate the work done by this man. To me, a pivot-maker was in a league of his own. I was attracted by the work done by Daniel Roth – since this is the man to I am referring. We talked and I then invited him to Viroflay, near Versailles where we lived. We had similar ideas regarding the great name of Breguet, so I asked the Chaumet to hire him and the adventure began. Daniel Roth is an exceptional watchmaker with a wonderful mindset!

For two years, Jacques Reymond, a professor at the Watchmaking School of Le Sentier in the Vallée de Joux, taught him the ins and outs of "grandes complications" in watchmaking. He subsequently became the technical director at Breguet in the Vallée de Joux.

In November 1976, we hired Louis-Maurice Caillet, a highly cultured man, a true genius in the realm of watchmaking and a perfectly accurate prototype maker, who still works for Breguet today, 40 years on!

Breguet BA 3050
Perpetual Calendar
Photo: Antiquorum

Daniel Roth and Louis-Maurice Caillet were a promising duo. Having them on board immediately positioned Breguet at a highly technical level. Although the brand was being introduced to the market, I wanted the idea of excellence to be immediately imprinted on connoisseurs' minds. We needed to start with a powerful image.

For these two watchmakers, the adventure was going to be a truly amazing challenge! We hired a room at the Vallée de Joux Technical College and work began in the first workshop which was small indeed, measuring barely 16m²!

The perpetual calendar was rare and very few were produced – a mere dozen or so worldwide, counting all all the brands together.

We decided to aim for a perpetual calendar indicating the months, days of the week, date and moon phases, as well the leap-year cycle, which represented a major technical feat. Daniel Roth and Louis-Maurice Caillet focused their efforts on producing this watch. They were the only people in the workshop and they were also responsible for the purchase or production of all parts and supplies. Completely alone in drawing the plans, making the prototypes, buying the machines, machining certain parts from steel before filing and assembling them, they really had to be extremely passionate about that they were doing. Everything was hand-made. A perpetual calendar required 50 steel parts and stars, 34 screws, 60 pins, eight studs, eight pipes… not to mention the 180 parts of the movement

CHAUMET S.A.

Breguet

ECOLE TECHNIQUE DU SENTIER
LE SENTIER 1348
Tél. : 021-85-49-59

CHAUMET S.A. – Breguet stamp
Le Sentier Technical College, 1976

itself. Some 30 different professions were required to make these components – all for just a single watch.

We only produced two or three perpetual calendars a year in the beginning, so we were not trying to make a profit on this product. Well aware that it takes a brand 15 years to become known, we set ourselves the primary objective of achieving excellence. This is how Breguet launched the fashion for complicated watches.

I opted to reserve the sale of these perpetual calendars for "Les Temporelles Chaumet" shop on the Place Vendôme, at least initially. For this reason, I took the decision to set the sales price at double that of other brands. High Jewellery clients bought each piece at this price, which meant that Breguet re-emerged within a purely jewellery context. I positioned

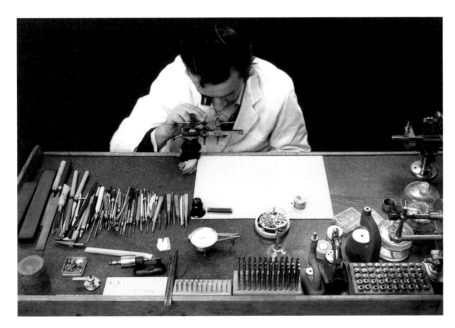

Jean-Louis Sautebin, one of the early watchmakers

the brand at the very top of the pyramid and clients regarded a Breguet watch as a piece of jewellery.

In parallel to manufacturing these pieces, cushion- and oval-shaped watches were also produced by the workshop. Despite the small numbers produced, there was an incredible variety of silvered or gold dials; while others featured a centre paved with diamonds, lapis lazuli, tiger's eye, onyx and even coral. The exterior was often silvered or gold and hand-guillochéd. Guillochage, otherwise referred to by Breguet as 'hand-engraving on a rose engine' or 'engine-turning', is an art that involves decorating the surface of the dial with engraved, intersecting lines. The caseband was also fluted by hand.

Louis-Maurice Caillet designed prototypes of classical and openworked perpetual calendars in addition to all the exterior elements required for production. Based on these designs, Daniel Roth, who was soon supported by a small team, produced small miracles.

Simple, ultra-thin and openworked watches required slimming down the hands over their entire length in order for them to be introduced between the glass and the dial. This was Louis-Maurice Caillet's job, as was the manual finish of the tips of the hands.

Once complete, the orders needed to be processed, which Louis-Maurice Caillet did on a corner of his drawing table! In truth, Daniel Roth and Louis-Maurice Caillet worked on miracles of time-keeping with never a thought for their own time!

By 1977, we had to increase production of perpetual calendars due to strong demand. This meant hiring a very skilled watchmaker. I discussed this with the Chaumet brothers who didn't wish to employ anybody else at this time. As a result, I suggested giving part of my salary to enable this hire to take place. Seeing my determination, they finally agreed to take an outstanding watchmaker, Jean-Louis Sautebin, onto the Breguet team without touching my pay. I think they were surprised by this determination on the part of a salaried employee who was willing to put his own income on the line in order to hire somebody for the good of the company – and this convinced them to go ahead.

Breguet was clearly on the up and up. The team moved to the ground floor of a house In Le Brassus. Four years later, the second floor was also occupied, prior to the entire house being bought by the Chaumet brothers. Denys Capt took over the administrative side of Breguet and was indispensable to the good management of the company! A native of the Vallée, he knew the people of the region, who also knew him, resulting in mutual trust which enabled both acceptance and excellent collaboration.

My wish was for the senior artisans to be surrounded by several younger ones in each workshop. I felt it was vital that their precious know-how should not vanish with them, but instead that their professional expertise and experience should represent both a legacy and a source of education for the younger generation.

Production of the Type XX ceased with the arrival of perpetual calendars.
Photo: Antiquorum

From my watchmaking past, I had a lot of respect for the work of these skilled men, who were meticulous, creative and passionate. Our many discussions meant I got to know them better, a process that consolidated my convictions regarding the strategy to be implemented. Talking with them constantly revealed new facets of this art, which in turn facilitated my marketing presentation and enabled me to quite naturally convey the Breguet mindset to clients. The "early watchmakers" were the main driving force behind Breguet.

During the first years of "Les Temporelles Chaumet", Breguet sold to the Indian, Belgian, Israeli and French military its Type XI onboard chronometers for their planes

and Type XX wristwatches for their pilots. These pieces were part of the existing Breguet stock. The arrival of the perpetual calendars placed luxury watches and "cheap" items shoulder to shoulder, a situation that seemed to me to be damaging for the brand image. I thereby put to a stop to all manufacturing and sales of the Type XX and Type XI models on the Breguet sales networks.

Much later, when Breguet's image was solidly established, I re-started the production of Type XX wrist chronographs within a Marine line.

It appeared to me that we were well-placed in the Vallée de Joux, far from the hustle and bustle of city life and the temptation to indulge in greed-driven excesses. Switzerland provided great advantages with the remarkable quality of its watchmakers and very peaceful working conditions.

I think one anecdote clearly demonstrates this very tangible atmosphere. More than 20 years ago, Marcel Calame, our case manufacturer, called upon a specialist who made gold ingots. The man used to ride all over La Chaux-de-Fonds by bicycle, transporting his precious cargo – meaning the gold ingots (!) – on the carrier. He had no hesitation in stopping at a café for a quick cup of coffee. His bicycle remained on the pavement as did the gold with no particular surveillance apart from the odd glance he gave it! What a wonderful era!

Marcel Calame made Breguet's most beautiful cases entirely by hand, infusing Breguet watches with incomparable authenticity and style. By the same token, the hand-guillochéd dials of the Stern company in Geneva represented admirable feats of manual craftsmanship.

To ensure the Vallée maintained direct contact with Paris, I had invited my team of watchmakers to visit Chaumet. I thought it would be a good thing if they could immerse themselves in the atmosphere of the Place Vendôme, with the large salon, the shops, and the High Jewellery workshops. They were hosted by the Chaumet brothers and both parties

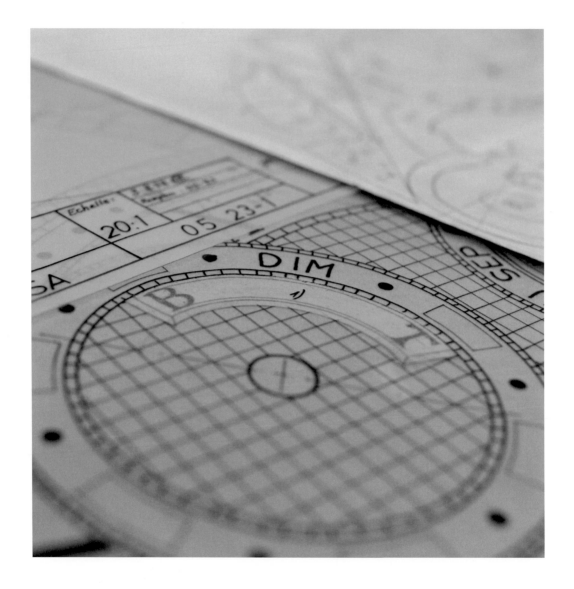

valued the opportunity to exchange views. Things you know and understand always make better sense…

Between Le Brassus and Paris, different temperaments and mindsets had to work together and thus trust each other. As far as I was concerned, we had not yet achieved everything we wanted to in the Vallée de Joux. I had heard of a certain Daniel Jeanrichard, a 90 year-old retired army colonel who smoked a pipe, lived with his white dog and cut a colourful figure. Whenever I visited Switzerland, I went to see him. Working from ebauches, he made perpetual calendars for Breguet and Chaumet clocks. His advanced age was inciting him to retire at last.

It was not easy for me as a stranger to gain his trust: only after three months of meetings and discussions did he finally open up his treasure chests. He had many tools and movements that I wanted to buy from him, but I was beaten to it by a Swiss competitor who had visited in between and taken everything.

Parallel to our production, and in the course of time, we had begun the restoration of historical pieces, a task performed by Louis Dumas, an exceptional watchmaker in Paris.

Paul-André Golay had joined our team of watchmakers in 1981 and was responsible for rewinding Piguet movements. The 70P was the basis of our deliberate policy for all "complication" and "ultra-thin" models, an approach that was both a political and a technical choice. Political because each watch had the same basic technical identity. Once wound up and perfectly adjusted by Paul-André Golay's team, this ultra-thin self-winding movement worked admirably and was one of the most beautiful movements in production.

In order to guarantee the precision of the 70P, Paul-André Golay worked in close collaboration with Louis Dumas to evaluate the pieces emerging from the company workshops after six months of "wearing".

While creating new watches is the focal point involving a lot of challenges, restoration also has its share of excellence which deserves appropriate recognition. Restoring means

Louis-Maurice Caillet
in front of his technical drawings
for horological complications.

doing everything possible to ensure that a broken or spoilt piece retains its style, shape and original look, while making it run again. This is very delicate work and sometimes requires cutting or turning a new piece in old metals.

The brand was reborn, infused with a jeweller's mindset. I clung passionately to this idea: a Breguet is a three-carat diamond! Selling a watch like this was like selling a library, a history with its finest watchmakers, a technique involving making very elaborate parts: a veritable treasure. In my opinion, Breguet's watchmakers were the equivalent of the jewellery specialists known as *premières mains* (premier hands): artisans capable of making necklaces, jewellery sets and diadems from start to finish.

During the first half of the 1980s, Breguet had re-edited old models with a power-reserve indicator completed by the date and moon phases, which were a perfect and entirely contemporary reflection of Breguet's style and a flagship embodiment of its expertise.

Milestone-shaped Breguet skeleton-movement mantel clocks in a workshop overlooking Le Brassus.

Over time, the range was enhanced with a milestone-shaped mantel clock, an openworked movement, a perpetual calendar with a power reserve, an off-centred watch and a Marine clock on which our watchmakers from the Vallée de Joux had worked.

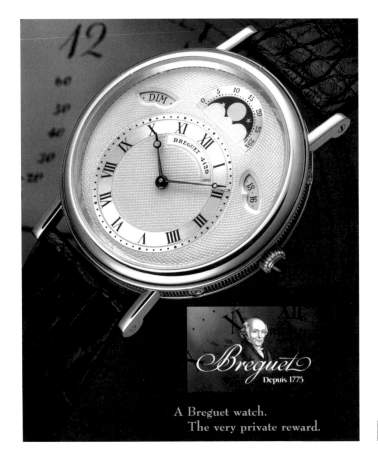

Breguet yellow gold self-winding off-centred model – 1982

When he made the skeleton mantel clock, Louis-Maurice Caillet had received the rough movement which he did not find appealing and regarded with a degree of scepticism, wondering how best to work with it. He took his compass and in three or four strokes, he found the solution! Intuition had kicked in! Intuition and talent…

My lucky break as a jeweller, when introducing Breguet to the market, was to be able to do so via the House of Chaumet whose prestige boosted the retail price of the watches. Fifty or a hundred thousand Swiss francs are common sums in the world of jewellery. Breguet aligned its prices with those of precious stones.

When perpetual calendars started to come onto the market, I made the decision to sell a Breguet at double the price of the competitor brands. The worst disasters were predicted and some people could already see our downfall! Nothing like that occurred! I considered this Breguet, which was mainly sold to Chaumet's jewellery clients, as a true gem.

Breguet in 1977 amid its snow-covered setting in Le Brassus, Vallée de Joux – Switzerland.

The "early watchmakers" were the main driving force behind Breguet

A few watchmaking professions

Constructor	Index maker
Technical draughtsman	Hand maker
Calibre specialist (micromechanic)	Dial maker
Balance-spring maker	Glass maker
Balance-wheel maker	Seal maker
Escapement maker	Case maker
Spring maker	Crown and pushpiece maker
Ebauches maker	Bracelet maker
Automatic lathe setter	Lug maker
Pinion maker	Electroplating operator
Wheel maker	Decorator specialised in
Polisher	watch pieces
Beveller	Mechanic
Jewel maker	Swage maker
Shock-absorber maker	

The distinctive features of a Breguet:
Caseband fluting
Engine-turned dials
Hands and numerals
Distinctive lugs
Individual number
Secret signature

CHAPTER 5

TIFFANY AND THE RISE OF BREGUET

Around 1981-1982, Breguet's rise and the expansion of its renown across the world were a constant focus. It was a rare brand, known only to a circle of initiates. I like to say that it takes a few minutes to sell a Rolex in the United States, between 15 and 20 minutes to sell another famous brand, and three-quarters of an hour to sell a Breguet! That is the time it takes to explain its history and its qualities – all that contributes to its incomparable worth.

At that time, there was a need to increase the number of watchmakers, focus on international marketing, raise brand awareness and sell the brand across the world.

The "pure jewellery" mindset was firmly ingrained in the ranks of top management at Tiffany's – the quintessential New York luxury company – which had a similar policy to mine.

For a certain number of years, the names of Tiffany and Breguet appeared on the dials of watches. This was not easy, since Chaumet regarded Tiffany as an international competitor. But because the latter enabled me to sell a large number of watches every year, the economic arguments outweighed the rest… This move marked a step towards Breguet becoming independent of Chaumet.

In the USA, I found a solution to help promote the brand thanks to a banker friend in New York, who was number two in a New York high-society club. A great collector of pocket watches of which he owned more than 2,000, he opened the doors of the club which placed at my disposal a room and a library overlooking 5th Avenue that became a wonderful haven. The arrangement enabled me to rub shoulders with influential people and when I asked for an appointment with a store, I would write on paper bearing the club letterhead, a procedure that proved highly effective and ensured a prompt welcome! This phase proved pivotal in helping emancipate Breguet from Chaumet and the club was a magnificent opportunity for the brand. I lived there during my stays in New York. Initially exclusively male, it subsequently opened its doors to women and my wife was able to accompany me.

This laid the foundation for a number of contacts that were to give the brand the boost I was seeking. Many success stories depend on our foresight at a given moment – an intuition that comes at the right time. Passion remained the ever-present driving force on the path towards new achievements.

Professional relationships, the missions to which fresh challenges led, and objectives to be met, did not prevent discoveries and friendships. I remember one particular day when I was visiting the basements of the Smithsonian Museum in Washington, a fabulous treasure trove packed with collector's items. Just when I least expected it, someone brought me a magnificent, delicious "Black Forest" cake to celebrate my birthday which fell on that day! A true pleasure that delighted me and a gesture that I found particularly touching.

One of my key roles at Chaumet was the responsibility for certain external markets, and particularly Japan. I was asked to handle jewellery in the Far East and I took part in the creation of the Chaumet Corners in Japan, with the support of Mitsukoshi, one of the most luxurious department store chains in the country with some 11-12,000 employees.

I brought together a hundred or so Japanese ladies from the highest social echelons in their country and presented the Chaumet High Jewellery collections. I also organised shows with fashion models wearing Chaumet's most beautiful sets. Because I wore two hats, Chaumet and Breguet, I was indirectly able to position Breguet at the highest level.

Breguet, Les Temporelles and the jewellery with which I was involved: from Chaumet's standpoint, it was good to have me active on several fronts at once.

Japan is not a country one can instantly grasp and I only really started understanding it on my sixth or seventh visit. In Asia, there are no individual responsibilities and it was essential to work on the staff as a whole in order to have an impact on the numerous employees. I sometimes brought 500 salespeople together, for example, and presented Chaumet High Jewellery to the entire gathering. I had not targeted the top of the pyramid

– the senior management – but instead the base, these 500 employees. The impact and the brand awareness were instantly greater.

Nonetheless, this policy did not completely explain the welcome success encountered in Japan. I had wondered for a long time why the Japanese had accepted me so easily. What was behind this, the real reason? I was aware that in one respect I resembled them: my diminutive stature was an advantage! This characteristic facilitated a certain integration, a physical identity akin to their own. I did not tower over them, we stood eye to eye, without one of us having to look down and the other crane their neck. It might not sound like much, but something which might seem merely incidental actually proved a major factor in fostering mutual exchanges and trust-building – and hence a key business asset.

The success encountered was such that a manga describing the history of Breguet and the challenge I had taken up was created and published in the very well-known Japanese magazine, *Begin*, in summer 2006 (see pp. 111 and onwards).

My involvement with Chaumet also allowed me to promote Breguet, in a subtle political game based on tacit agreement. Within the company on Place Vendôme, I was one of the only employees amongst the 250-strong contingent who was able to travel all over the world without needing to ask permission. The turnover I brought in was fairly considerable, although it did not entitle me to ask for a salary increase… Longevity was the only thing that counted. That was the problem on Place Vendôme! In the eyes of the employees who had been with the company for 30 years, young Bodet still had a long way to go!

So there we were. The only option was to keep to my allotted place, while remaining obstinate. I was stubbornly determined to make Breguet one of the greatest brands in the world.

I had learnt many things during my apprenticeship with my father and some had remained vividly imprinted on my memory, such as the Rolex mindset which was part and parcel of the brand that my father had represented since 1950.

Their way of doing things always consisted of choosing the bourgeoisie in each city as their custodians: in other words, people who were respected within a circle of 50,000 to 100,000 people. I wished to apply this system in turn with Breguet. If a brand is sold by people who are respected, the product is necessarily also respected.

I was aware that, more than 80 years earlier, Breguet had worked with Bugatti, notably by producing the Bugatti Royale watch, of which seven had been made. This idea pleased me! What a great partnership! Someone who collects cars collects watches… At least potentially! We were by then into the 1990s, so why not renew such ties? I had had the opportunity of getting to know Lamborghini… where hand craftsmanship ruled as it did on Breguet models. I went to Bologna, managed to obtain an interview with the director and was not in his office for long before he sent me on my way! I was just leaving when, quite by chance, I bumped into the test driver. I described my vision to him, my idea, the value I could see in it. A few hours later, at lunchtime, I was eating with the Chairman, who didn't reject the project! Louis-Maurice Caillet designed the prototype with the Lamborghini logo on a gold dial, intended for the Diablo. This hand-wound chronograph was sold for the price of a 2CV.

The first dial proposed was round but did not appear to please the technical director who suggested a square shape. If that were the only issue, it could be easily settled and we did just that! During a cocktail party in Monaco, the Lamborghini Diablo was presented with its Breguet dashboard counter. It was a good-looking package!

It had been agreed that the model would be launched and presented at the Geneva Car Show. The lead times were a bit short and Louis-Maurice Caillet remembers having had to take the train to ensure that, the day before the official opening, which was media day, the counter could be installed on a sumptuous yellow Lamborghini Diablo.

You have to be persistent when fighting for a cause you believe in.

When clients visiting the Place Vendôme asked me to give them a discount and I felt I could, I would do a quick mental calculation and express it to them in the form of a metaphor they could identify with: "There we are, it amounts to the same thing as a return trip from Paris to New York." The client could thus understand the value of what was being given to them.

Still driven by this desire to provide Breguet with a name and a reputation in its own right, independent of the Chaumet influence, I decided to present the brand at the 1983 edition of the Basel Fair. I had a little booth beneath the escalator. It was appropriate to remain modest and to accept our assigned place.

The start of marketing was an important stage for the brand. Breguet needed to grow and this was my responsibility as the only "salesperson". I was asked to give a lecture at the *Musée International d'Horlogerie* in La Chaux-de Fonds and I was aware that a presentation of this kind could have a considerable impact.

At the time, neither Pierre and Jacques Chaumet, nor the financial director at the time, agreed with my policy of exploiting the name of Breguet on its own, outside of Chaumet's sphere of influence. I was in a difficult position and I needed to know how far I could go. However, my perseverance reaped rewards and I received a number of orders at Basel 1983, as well as gaining a number of pioneering international agents such as Helmut Teriet for Germany, Giovanni Sutti for Italy and of course, Albert Hausamann for Hong Kong. All of them made a considerable contribution to Breguet's culture and played an effective part in the brand's expansion in Europe and Asia.

Prior to the Basel experience, we were still small, selling 500 to 700 timepieces a year of which 50% within the Chaumet group. It was difficult to find people who believed in Breguet. Chaumet was an essential support. I never did anything without feeling immense respect for the House of Chaumet. It must be emphasised that respect was an integral part of the Place Vendôme mindset, where luxury was not confined to appearances.

I was fortunate enough to be able to count on a number of excellent retailers and to have met key personalities, to whom I was fairly close, such as Frédy Jean-Jacquet, director of "Les Ambassadeurs" boutique in Geneva; Theodor Beyer, a major watch owner and collector, with an amazing museum in Zurich; Jürg Kirchhofer of Interlaken; Koenig d'Ambassy in Lucerne and Kurt Schindler in Zermatt. I worked directly with them and enjoyed the benefit of their teaching.

Amongst other influential characters was Henri Marquis, journalist, writer and publisher of the *Swiss Watch Journal* and *Challenge*, who always gave the Breguet brand a place of honour in its publications. Not to mention André Curtit, professor at the Watchmaking School of Chaux-de-Fonds, and curator of the International Museum in the same town, who was also a valuable contact. After more than 40 years of passion dedicated to the museum and the acquisition of more than 1,000 pieces during the course of his career, he retired and was thanked for his services with a ridiculously small sum allocated by the municipality.

An hour later, I decided to hire him as our curator, with the job of buying the brand's old watches, evaluating them and producing certificates for each of the pieces. It was both thanks to and through him that in the 1980s I was introduced to Jean-Pierre Savary, President of the Watchmakers of Switzerland Information Center in New York. Swiss watchmakers wishing to launch in the United States naturally sought advice from him. He was a key figure who gave Breguet a lot of excellent publicity in the USA.

Messrs Curtit, Jean-Jacquet, Beyer and Marquis were all renowned characters and experienced individuals able to provide highly relevant advice. Their presence and prestige enabled me to expand Breguet's culture as "an old name and young brand" on the international watchmaking scene.

Over the following years, I revived the presence of a Breguet booth at the Basel Fair, where it has annually exhibited ever since. From its insignificant position under the staircase, and in keeping with the spirit of the brand's international representation, Breguet had now won a prime spot.

I was keen to reveal the prestige of the Breguet brand. It became clear that the best possible proof could be provided by exhuming historical treasures and exhibiting them so that people could appreciate their beauty, elegance and technical sophistication. All the speeches in the world would not have the same powers of persuasion as simply contemplating these marvels.

Through the intermediary of André Curtit and Théodore Beyer, private collections including that of Thomas Engels, the Breguet collection and pieces from the *Musée International d'Horlogerie*, as well as a number of pieces from the Rolex Museum, were gathered and prepared to set out on a mission to elicit wonderment: 50 historical watches, some of Breguet's finest creations, were to be presented to the public.

The Chaumet boutique on London's Bond Street was the first stop on the journey (September 4th to 20th 1986), with nine windows featuring blue velvet backgrounds providing the perfect setting for watches which were reflected in mirrors in the back so as to display a detail, a movement or an engraving. These wonders included the Duke of Wellington's superb pocket watch. London high society came to admire these rare pieces as well as recent models from the new Breguet collection, veritable gems and true embodiments of the historical Breguet watches exhibited.

An audio-visual presentation featuring a perfect kaleidoscope of images told the tale of Breguet on two screens, accompanied by 18th century music. The overall effect was completely in harmony with the era!

After London came Geneva in the Chaumet boutique on the Rue du Rhône (September 25th – October 9th 1986). A painting on loan from the Château de Penthes

(Geneva) – the *Musée des Suisses à l'étranger* (Museum of the Swiss abroad) – provided another presentation for all those interested.

People waited on three floors to see the audio-visual presentation of the collection of historical watches from the *Musée International de l'Horlogerie* (MIH) in la Chaux-de-Fonds and the private collections. The exhibition had chosen to accompany the beauty of the watches with an everyday object from a given era – a cup of tea, a golf ball, a book, opera glasses...

There was also a chance to admire marine chronometers, including a modern chronometer in its mahogany casket.

One of the "three-wheel" clocks made by subscription at the MIH restoration centre was beautifully displayed under a glass dome.

And then came Paris (October 14th to 31st 1986), where Breguet was hosted in style, naturally on the Place Vendôme. Presented on two floors, pieces from the collection were accompanied by a great many documents. In the salons, enlarged with mirrors, the collections were displayed to splendid effect.

No less than 600 guests were invited to the cocktail party and held in "Grand Siècle" (17th century) style under the large crystal chandeliers and candlesticks placed on the two fireplaces in the Grand Salon.

The audio-visual presentation appeared on two separate screens in the middle of the Chaumet Museum, and amongst other things, included the collection of crowns made over 200 years by the House of Chaumet.

After a magnificent detour to New York (November 5th to 22nd 1986) and Brussels (November 27th to December 9th 1986), the exhibition returned to the Maison Beyer in Zurich on December 15th 1986.

The Breguet workshops in Le Brassus had thus been presented in London as well as Geneva, New York, Brussels and Paris, telling the tale of this noble adventure of watches representing veritable treasures. Behind these creations are men and women… Without the excellent work of the watchmakers, the incredible thrill of discovery they procure simply would not exist.

Pierre Chaumet had emphasised: "A Breguet watch single-handedly represents true technical progress by uniting the meaning of French beauty with Swiss technique to create a truly timeless pleasure."

This great round of exhibitions gave Breguet a huge boost through the revelation of its history and the presentation of historical watches. In marketing terms, it was a fantastic operation for Chaumet which allowed it to establish the brand's reputation and impact sales. It was at this time that the Chaumet fully grasped Breguet's potential, with a pleasure tinged with concern at the shadow cast by the success that this name was becoming.

This success was forged by a number of skilled hands! I have already mentioned some of the meaningful encounters with André Curtit and Théodore Beyer, but I also wish to pay tribute to the watchmakers of Le Brassus – to Louis-Maurice Caillet, Paul-André Golay, Daniel Roth, and his wife Nicole, who filled a thousand roles. They had a difficult mission and a thankless job before gradually managing to surround themselves with other capable individuals. In Paris, my assistant Anne Fabien, an enthusiastic person who was passionate about the Breguet brand and subsequently became director of marketing in France, along with Louis Dumas, were also invaluable.

Our strength lay in our tightly knit team. My four-year apprenticeship enabled me to understand the problems encountered by employees, to talk to them knowledgeably and feel close to them – not as a Business School graduate but as a craftsman. I was the only ex-apprentice to serve as CEO of a brand, a fact that enabled me to have an insider view of the world of watchmaking and a certain kinship with those who worked in it.

According to Louis-Maurice Caillet, who was from the Vallée de Joux, Swiss watchmaking was at its lowest ebb in 1976. Breguet's arrival meant that little by little, the

Vallée de Joux became a watchmaking centre of key importance… A certain dynamic was gaining momentum, drawing in its wake the establishment of new brands and the revival of small workshops. This new boom was good for everyone and in particular the inhabitants of the Vallée.

After Breguet's first appearance in Basel in 1983, our concern was to fan the Breguet flame ever brighter. During 1987-1988, we began to study the famous "Breguet Tourbillon" created in 1795 and patented on June 26th 1801 (7 Messidor of year IX according to the French revolutionary calendar), a date which we engraved on the mainplate. The tourbillon was a new device at the time which cancelled the effects of earth's gravity by means of its constant rotation. It took no less than three years of research before re-launching it in 1990. It represented the pinnacle of Breguet's genius and was an iconic piece for this great watchmaker and for watchmaking in general.

The passion for watches – objects with limitless ability to fascinate – was equally strong among watchmakers as among collectors and clients… There were even collectors who got together every leap year between February 28th and 29th and March 1st, all wearing their Audemars Piguet, Patek or Breguet; at exactly midnight, with their gaze firmly fixed on their dial, they all watched to see if their timepieces jumped precisely to the next day's date! In short – a contest of accuracy!

I was obstinately determined to make Breguet one of the greatest brands in the world.

CHAPTER 6
OCCUPATIONAL HAZARDS

Modesty is undoubtedly a good characteristic to cultivate in this trade. Given the incredible high stakes and exorbitant sums involved, discretion and caution are must-have qualities, while a taste for taking risks and travelling is also useful!

One day, when I was visiting Tiffany's in New York with the collection, the plane's engine caught fire in the middle of the Atlantic. We lost altitude and the pilot turned back and landed in Paris. Three-quarters of an hour later, I took off again, having asked the Administrative Director not to say anything to my family. The result of all that was that instead of arriving in New York at 7pm, it was midnight when the plane landed on the tarmac at the airport. This meant I was at considerable risk. I had the collection with me and after going through the border checks, the customs officials wanted to order me a taxi. I refused…it was up to me to decide… they had seen the collection and I needed to be careful!

When I reached my hotel, I found a bouquet of flowers from Chaumet accompanied by a note. Given my employee status, this gave me immense pleasure!

It was, however, all too painfully obvious that the secretary of the House of Chaumet did not much like me and did whatever she could to make me pay the price. Her role was to make hotel reservations for me when I travelled. One day, I arrived in Hong Kong and was driven to a complete dump in the suburbs. She was well acquainted with the town and knew exactly what she was doing. I had the Breguet collection with me. It rained in my room but I said nothing and went about my business.

During an executive meeting, after I was appointed head of jewellery in Japan, certain committee members asked Chaumet to relieve me of these responsibilities. They knew nothing about me or what I had achieved and studied, but they were stirred by jealousy and envy. It was of key importance that I negotiate this hazard that effectively made them my enemies, while not trying to get above myself. I believed in what I was doing and was aware of making pioneering progress. I brought in money for the group, which was tangible evidence of my effectiveness, to the point where the Chaumet brothers had even asked me to go to Tokyo for the sole purpose of attending a dinner.

On another occasion, in order to sign a contract with Tiffany in New York, Pierre Chaumet and I did the return trip by Concorde in a single day.

I knew that the people who counted valued me, which was enough for me to remain silent and ignore the dreaded envious brigade. Through the intermediary of André Curtit and Théodore Beyer, I met people who collected Breguet watches. This was a fantastic help in enhancing my knowledge of the brand as well as enhancing its renown, since documents and written evidence were few and far between and generally inadequate.

It had been suggested to me that a Milan-based retailer, a truly admirable man, knew everything there was to know about Breguet. I travelled from Geneva to meet him and become acquainted, taking a grey suitcase with me. I had got used to keeping one foot on my suitcase all the time as a sort of automatic professional response. When I reached the customs in Milan, there was another grey suitcase next to mine. Somebody was trying to take mine. I was driven to the retailer where he immediately warned me that I was being followed. He took out his gun and our entire discussion took place with it on the table! When it was time to leave, he showed me out through a side door.

Tenacity in the face of adversity, determination in whatever one undertakes: I regard these values as indispensable in overcoming any obstacles one may encounter.

For about three weeks, I experienced a debilitating health problem in the form of a sort of spinal paralysis that severely restricted my mobility. Nevertheless, I still had things to do, including going to Tiffany's where I was organising exhibitions. My collection was not the only thing I took to New York. my wheelchair came too! I privately felt it was an excellent way of travelling in complete safety. I was so ably supported by my wife – my faithful companion – as well as other helpers, that it would have been impossible to make an attempt on what I was transporting.

I held a cocktail party or two at the Plaza on 5th Avenue, fortunately organised and supervised by my wife who helped me enormously. Once this was done, I travelled to other cities in the United States, and to Tiffany's where I welcomed clients in a wheelchair.

Little by little, I replaced the chair with crutches. The time came for me to sign my first agent's contract in Hong Kong. I took the plane in Los Angeles, complete with my two precious crutches! From Hong Kong, I had to go on to Tokyo where I felt better – so much better that I decided to leave my crutches in the taxi! I had circled the globe, starting off paralysed and in a wheel chair, progressing to crutches, and ending up on my own two feet! Driven by indestructible faith, I knew I would make it!

One day the Place Vendôme was burgled and several pieces of jewellery were stolen. "Les Temporelles" was also affected and a great many watches worth a lot of money disappeared. The court case took place in Vancouver and the Chaumet brothers asked me to be a witness.

I had barely arrived in Vancouver when I was surrounded by six well-built police officers who never left me alone for a second over the eight days I attended the case. When we weren't in court, we played cards with the mafia which had ordered the burglary because over there, as long as you have not been convicted, you are perfectly free!

In Japan in the 1980s, another mishap occurred. When I was head of Chaumet in this country, together with our partner Mitsukoshi, I organised a series of fashion parades featuring Chaumet jewellery. Each set was more beautiful than the last: diamond-set necklaces, earrings and assorted rings were elegantly worn by very beautiful young women before an 800-strong audience. The value of these magnificent objects was estimated at several tens of millions of Swiss francs. These shows were held in Japan's biggest cities and attended by Pierre Chaumet.

One day, after a show, I was returning to Paris via Amsterdam. At the border crossing, the customs officials asked to check my merchandise passport, unfortunately in full view of certain passengers! I took the plane headed to Paris-Charles De Gaulle where Security was waiting for me. But to my horror, the plane landed at Orly and I cannot begin to tell you the extent of my anxiety! Nobody was waiting for me and I was carrying goods worth an insane amount! Despite my cold sweats, everything went fine!

All these events made me realise I needed to be more careful! I could not allow myself to be lulled and weakened by comfort and all-encompassing luxury… I constantly had to remind myself of everything that had helped toughen me up through the various stages of my life.

Apart from that, these various incidents enabled Chaumet to give me free rein in complete confidence, safe in the knowledge that they could rely on me.

In the hectic life I led and which led me, it was important to find a place to recharge my batteries. Brittany brought me this with its sea, its land, its space and the immense sky above me! I let these natural elements infuse me with their energy and vitality, speaking to my solitude. I needed their presence both around and in me. When one is constantly surrounded by luxury, when an international activity tends to make us lose touch with ourselves, it is good to renew our harmony with the elements, which direct us to engage in inward reflection by putting the value and stature of all things into perspective. This brought me invaluable equilibrium without which I might have been at risk.

CHAPTER 7

1987 – A TURBULENT YEAR

In 1983, I had been appointed director of Breguet by Chaumet. I was naturally thrilled by this responsibility, since it represented both my own passion as well as the great trust that the Chaumet had already placed in me. However, despite apparent success, we were not yet out of the woods ...

In 1987, things were difficult for Chaumet, which was bearing the brunt of a tough economic environment. Jewellery ratings were down, the price of diamonds had crashed, and Breguet was the group's only thriving element. From the outside, we had no idea of the true extent of the problems and all kinds of vague rumours were swirling about. From an administrative perspective, Breguet was legally dependent on Chaumet as part of the same entity.

During that same year, the factory at Le Brassus was burgled. Finished pieces were taken and a large number of movements were trampled on, in an obviously criminal act.

Rumours of Chaumet going bankrupt were circulating fast, as they always do. Breguet owed a lot of money. The financial situation was extremely difficult, suppliers were not always paid, Chaumet could not meet its commitments and bankruptcy seemed imminent. At the beginning of Basel Fair, I had several millions' worth of orders but at the end, there was just one million!

I found a solution by contacting well-known retailers or importers who distributed Breguet. They demonstrated their trust in us and renewed their orders confidently in order to compensate for the pieces stolen from the Breguet workshops in Le Brassus, which saved us momentarily.

Daniel Roth had found three minute-repeater movements. Watchmakers from Breguet and others from another manufacturer had got together and gradually built these movements. Alas, amid the economic troubles that Chaumet was experiencing, Breguet had no money. Somebody came along, snapped them up and used these movements to launch their own brand!

Events continued to unfold in bleak succession. A bank that worked with the House of Chaumet and was confronted by the latter's difficulties seized a hundred or so finished pieces. This hamstrung situation continued to worsen for Chaumet.

Times were hard and disaster was looming... Everyone wanted Breguet but for as little as possible, and the apparently inevitably bankruptcy was a good way to achieve this! I tried everything in my power to avoid it. I would have loved Breguet to be acquired by Hermès or Boucheron, both of which belonged to the Comité Colbert, but that didn't happen, which was a great pity...

In August 1987, I had sensed that the archive books at the Place Vendôme in which all historical Breguet sales from yesteryear were recorded might disappear. These books are part of the brand heritage and were in my office. On August 12th, this premonition of the potential risk led me to call the President of the Commercial Court to ask him to place my office under surveillance. I was right to be suspicious...

While the storm continued to batter Chaumet, the Swiss Chamber of Commerce ordered an enquiry among all Breguet's suppliers to find out if they had been paid. None responded... They all trusted us and thanks to their support, the name of Breguet was not blackened in any way. Marcel Calame (cases) and André Colard (dials) from the Stern company (Geneva) even travelled to Viroflay, near Versailles, where we lived, to testify to the probity of our collaboration. A wonderful demonstration of trust!

The Commercial Court in Paris had taken control of all Chaumet and Breguet products, including the pieces we wore and which belonged to the brand. Consequently, I even had to return the power-reserve model that I had worn on my wrist right from the very beginning. Some time later, when the storm had blown over, the President of the Court would give it back to me. This took place in 1994 and a certificate testifies to this return in these terms: "Watch given to Mr François Bodet by the Paris Judicial Administration."

Meanwhile, we were still in big trouble! The Commercial Court decided to accept an offer from Investcorp group, which bought Chaumet and took control of the Breguet brand.

Requests had meanwhile been pouring into the Commercial Court. Interested parties wanted Breguet's watchmakers, clients, manufacturing capacities and certain suppliers… It was not however easy for anyone to try and poach my watchmakers, who were earning more than what all my competitors were offering. There was nothing very pretty about what was going on at that time!

This difficult period affected me. I knew I was being watched and I was aware of the desire of certain people to see Breguet bite the dust. My wife received many anonymous telephone calls, notably including repeated death threats and defamatory remarks insinuating that I had a mistress: a whole battery of attacks intended to silence me and inject their poison right into my private life. We were the victims of intense stress, even though my wife avoided telling me of these anonymous telephone calls, attempting to spare me as much as she could. I only found out about them later, once we were firmly established in Switzerland. She was severely depressed for several weeks, but we needed to pick ourselves up and continue helping Breguet out of its difficulties and onto the path to success.

During all the ups and downs, all the pitfalls and hard knocks, my wife Marie-Laure supported me unflinchingly. During the great Breguet adventure, she represented what no employee could ever have been: someone who supported my passion and believed in me when, during the darkest hours, I was assailed by doubt! Someone who was at my side with both elegance and simplicity, as well as with remarkable talent for human relations.

One evening in the spring of 1987, I went as I did every evening to have a chat in the Chaumets' office on the mezzanine overlooking the Place Vendôme. Pierre Chaumet asked me to remain standing. "Bodet," he said "Breguet's potential is becoming more important than Chaumet". I felt incredulous and was convinced that my last hour in the company had come. In reality, despite the fact that I had had virtually nothing with which to re-launch Breguet, the brand was achieving international renown. This enabled me to continue my task in keeping with the true Breguet spirit.

Thus, during a very turbulent 1987, our agents, retailers and suppliers retained their trust in my strategies, as did the entire Swiss and international Breguet team.

CHAPTER 8

BREGUET AFTER CHAUMET

Investcorp, the Anglo-American and Arab investment company, gave us a significant credit line. I spent part of the summer of 1987 with them at Saint-James, at Neuilly, in top-secret discussions. They wanted to understand Breguet's history, its path to date and the policy that I wished to follow. Convinced by what I told them, they advised me to move to Switzerland, a world far removed from business-related upheavals. This would position me right in the heart of watchmaking turf, which looked like a simpler option. The peaceful spirit in which everything took place here was a guarantee of quality.

We needed a policy that would ensure Breguet's development. In order to do this, I decided to hire a sub-contractor in the form of Parmigiani. This choice was a clear statement of my position of strength. It was all a matter of caution, and I was well aware that a lack of insight could erode even the most solid foundations. This external workshop added another string to our production bow.

In order to emphasise the importance of this issue and provide an explanatory nuance, it is worth pointing out that jewellery is 80% raw material and 20% manufacturing, while the ratio is reversed for watchmaking! The human resources issue therefore plays a decisive role.

Launched on a different basis, Breguet literally took off, with sales increasing from 1,200 to 4,700 units between 1987 and 1993.

In return for its considerable investment in Chaumet and Breguet, Investcorp expected good returns and significant financial endeavours. Marketing is a political science in its own right! Finding Breguet agents was a huge responsibility and there was no room for error! I received excellent advice from people at the head of large watch companies who pointed me in the right direction.

In 1992, my representative in Bahrain mentioned a remarkable man called Rodolphe Schulthess from Patek Philippe. He was the man for the job! One day when I was attending a cocktail party in Qatar, I met Philippe Stern, the big boss of Patek Philippe, and took the opportunity of presenting my request to him. He agreed, while asking me to wait six months.

The reasons I wanted at all costs to secure Rodolphe Schulthess' capabilities were of course based on his expertise, but also on his inherent elegance, which was a key factor. He fitted perfectly into the culture of Place Vendôme and reflected the atmosphere of the legendary company headquarters. The major changes Breguet had undergone had not diminished the fine jewellery-oriented spirit that lived on in the production team.

The situation was looking good, with a team of excellent watchmakers supported by the influence of the people I have just mentioned. Breguet was starting to be taken seriously. However, in order to break into Asia, we needed to consider a number of remarks that had been made to me such as "You only have a very small workshop in Le Brassus."

Several years went by before I had my agent in Hong Kong, who became my bridgehead to Asia.

While Breguet was already active in Japan, I was very keen to enter Hong Kong, which opened all doors to Asia.

Japan had a longstanding history in which refinement and elegance were sought-after values that inspired confidence. Elsewhere in Asia, other concepts prevailed and needed to be highlighted. Hong Kong was only totally convinced after the acquisition of Valdar, a manufacturer of micro-mechanics and watchmaking supplies, which employed a hundred or so people. As part of the same strategy, some time later, we also acquired Lemania, a manufacturer of movements for chronographs, complications, etc. – of which we were the second largest client.

Henceforth, we would no longer have to depend on movement manufacturers. The acquisition of Lemania gave us far greater autonomy and with this, we were able to call ourselves a Manufacture, a strictly regulated title which requires that virtually all production be undertaken by the same company.

The years had brought their different responsibilities with them, since I had successively served in various capacities:

- Manager of "Les Temporelles Chaumet", from 1975 to 1983.
- Project manager for the Breguet re-launch and head of the Chaumet jewellery business in Japan.
- Director of Breguet, appointed by Chaumet, from 1983 to 1987.
- Executive Director, appointed by Investcorp, from 1988 to 1991.
- Chairman of Breguet, appointed by Investcorp, from 1992 to 1996.

It had been a long road from the Angers railway station, where the little boy in grey overalls pulled his cart filled with packages, all the way to Place Vendôme …

CHAPTER 9

MARKETING

Louis Dumas had already joined Breguet in 1981. In addition to his initial function of repairing the brand's historical watches, he was charged with creating a connection between Paris and Le Brassus. When a watch was sold and had been worn by its new owner for six months, Louis Dumas took note of clients' opinions and passed them on to the watchmakers. This feedback put the watchmakers and clients in touch and enabled the former to continuously improve anything that required improvement. Breguet watches needed to be perfect to ensure that clients derived maximum enjoyment from wearing them. In addition, this feedback gave Breguet watchmakers well-deserved recognition for their work and their merits!

I always employed marketing agents who were capable of talking about Breguet for two or three hours. They were addressing specialised retailers who are cultured individuals naturally interested in selling, but whose main concern is to have prestigious products to present to their clients.

After the acquisition of Breguet by Investcorp, Wolfgang Peter, an attorney, was the designated intermediary for the shareholders of the Breguet Group. He provided extensive and ongoing support vis-à-vis our investors for the policy that we were pursuing for Breguet, as well as for that of the Group, eventually becoming CEO of the Group (Nouvelle Lemania, Valdar, Jaquet-Droz, Breguet).

Together with Wolfgang Peter, Yves Scherrer joined Breguet as Financial Director. He made a significant contribution to Breguet's administrative expansion in addition to that of the Group. He became Managing Director of Breguet when I was appointed Chairman. I subsequently hired Emmanuel Breguet, who was able to shed light on the history of Breguet.

In April 1991, a splendid auction was held in Geneva, with collectors and speculators vying for the lots on offer. Prices skyrocketed, starting for example with pieces such as a travel clock that belonged to Napoleon Bonaparte as well as a vintage wristwatch.

People had the impression that they were buying a piece of history

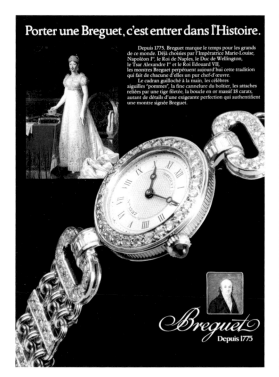

Others followed suit in a whirl of passionate enthusiasm. The total amount achieved by the sale was pretty impressive.

Jean-Claude Sabrier, an expert for Antiquorum, Geneva, accurately described the purchasers' mindset: "People had the impression that they were buying a piece of history."

I had never ceased doing whatever I could to reveal Breguet's prestige to the public, but this prodigious price explosion was mainly fuelled by an exhibition organised by Jean-Claude Sabrier of Antiquorum, under the auspices of Habsburg Fine Art Auctioneers.

Entitled "L'art de Breguet" (The art of Breguet), and retracing the history of the brand, this was held in the great palaces of the world: Paris (January 17th to 19th 1991); Milan (January 24th to 27th 1991); Munich (Janaury 31st to February 2nd 1991); London (February 6th to 9th 1991); New York (February 13th to 16th 1991); Los Angeles (February 20th to 23rd 1991); Tokyo (March 1st to 4th 1991); Hong Kong (March 14th to 17th 1991); Singapore (March 21st to 23rd 1991); Doha (March 27th and 28th 1991); and Geneva (April 11th to 13th 1991).

Breguet was now a point of reference in the realm of luxury watchmaking and its golden age had begun.

The premises at Le Brassus had long since become too small, and we had found additional space in other buildings around the Vallée de Joux, prior to buying the old file factory in L'Abbaye. In 1994, these freshly renovated and expanded buildings provided a new work environment in line with the image that the brand wished to present to the world. Henceforth, people spoke of the Manufacture Breguet in L'Abbaye! Once again, I must stress that this expansion would never have been possible without the support of our watchmakers, who were our greatest asset.

The collection was expanded and some 20 models were presented. After the power reserve came the perpetual calendar with a power reserve, within a case the same size as a perpetual calendar – an amazing feat by our watchmakers! Then came the *sympathique* clock exclusive to Breguet, in which the watch is fitted inside the clock that winds it and adjusts the time-setting, in temporal "sympathy"!

A Breguet stands out amongst a thousand other timepieces!

Yellow gold equation of time. Self-winding watch

Michel Caspar, formerly of Patek Philippe and who had now joined Breguet, began work on an equation of time "Grande Complication" model. He worked alone, creating parts entirely by hand in the old-fashioned way, and his achievement was a miracle!

Michel Caspar started with nothing but a steel plate, and the result was amazing! He trained two people to whom he passed on the quality and genius of this expertise. A few years later, we were producing more than 50 of these watches a year.

Buoyed up by and swept along in a wave of enthusiasm, points of sale were opening up all over the place. In 1987, there were around 70; five years later, in 1992, there were about 170, and by 1993, the number had shot up to 250. These excellent results attracted investors, so our objective had been successfully reached, although not without taking risks. Demand was so great that clients sometimes had to wait three years to receive their Breguet.

The Manufacture Breguet built on the old file factory at L'Abbaye, Vallée de Joux in 1994.
Photo: V. Jaton

Whatever the circumstances Breguet watches retained and still retain their five distinctive signs: the steel hollow, eccentric "moon" tip hands which are flame-blued at more than 300°C, the engine-turned dial and the fluted caseband with roller-type lugs and screw-in buckles. Like all rare pieces, each watch is numbered. Much had changed for our watchmakers but the quality of their work remained constant, meaning that a Breguet stood out amongst a thousand other timepieces!

In 1996, Wolfgang Peter, Yves Scherrer and I decided to set up a partnership to re-launch the Jaquet-Droz brand that I had acquired in 1987. We were able to rely on support in this endeavour from Rodolphe Schultess and Damien Source. We thus revived the prestigious name of Jaquet-Droz, notably with the manufacture of automatons in collaboration with François Junod, at Sainte-Croix.

In 2000, Jaquet-Droz was sold to Nicolas Hayek, who had bought Breguet the previous year. These two brands were and still are in very good hands. Nicolas Hayek had unquestionable flair and the quality and renown of these two prestigious brands would serve him well.

Breguet currently has more than 1,000 employees and between Breguet, Jaquet-Droz and the sub-contractors, several thousand families enjoy the benefit of this excellent position, which is a source of great satisfaction to me in terms of the jobs thus provided!

Marine chronometer,
hand-engraved
skeleton movement.
Rock crystal and gold.

CHAPTER 10

BREGUET AND HIS MAJESTY THE KING OF MOROCCO

Between 1986 and 2000, I made a number of trips to Morocco. His Majesty, Hassan II, King of Morocco, would call me and I would hop on a plane because he wanted to select the watches he wished to give his famous visitors.

I had met him for the first time in the 1980s. He had a great appreciation for the House of Chaumet with which he had established both trust and friendship. Pierre Chaumet enjoyed a special relationship with the king and I inherited this when I was responsible for Breguet.

Often when I was in his presence, he asked my point of view regarding his personal collections and on the pieces exhibited in his museums. I was at his entire disposal all day and most of the night. My availability was such that even at the swimming pool, I never swapped my business suit for my swimming costume, prepared for the smallest indication that I should meet with the king and thereby sure not to keep him waiting!

I was called into his private offices, often late at night. His Majesty knew that I was at his disposal and trusted me. He wanted us to create watchmaking pieces exclusively for him. The fact that King Hassan II gave his illustrious guests Breguet watches was a favour that was excellent for the brand's reputation and positioned it in the upper echelons.

Depending on the circumstances, I was accompanied by André Curtit, curator of the *Musée International d'Horlogerie* in La Chaux-de-Fonds, whose knowledge was respected by the heads of museums in Morocco.

In the 1990s, I asked Damien Source to accompany me. He belonged to Breguet's minute repeater department and was a former student of André Curtit. He was also a fully trained clockmaker, which was essential when it came to Morocco.

He was also discreet, respectful, well-educated, modest and patient – all essential qualities in a royal court. I knew I could rely on him and his extensive knowledge of complicated watches and clocks. His abilities were known to the Royal Palace and his job was to look after the clocks in the King's personal museum, as well as those in the Palace.

I had discovered a well-developed sense of marketing in Damien Sourice and later on he accompanied me, together with Rodolphe Schulthess, in creating Jaquet-Droz watches.

At the Royal Palace I was sometimes asked to do somewhat unpredictable things, which bore no relation to my profession, but I was there to be available to and to serve His Majesty. I must emphasise that the latter's knowledge in the realm of high-end watchmaking and jewellery was impressive and my answers had to make the grade.

Whenever I was called by His Majesty King Hassan II, my stay always began with a visit to the Royal Secretariat, even before seeing the King. This was the way of finding out if I was still welcome in His Majesty's "ante-chamber".

Being accepted by His Majesty King Hassan II for years was very good for Breguet – and subsequently for Jaquet-Droz. Not only did I achieve substantial sales, but I also knew that these watches were worn by the King's illustrious guests to whom he offered them as a token of welcome. My advisory relationship with the King represented considerable international leverage.

Mantel clock.
Lapis lazuli and yellow gold,
skeleton movement

CHAPTER 11

DEVELOPING THE GAME RULES OF MY BREGUET POLICY

W hen Jacques and Pierre Chaumet entrusted me with the task of awakening the Breguet brand from its long sleep, I had to implement projects, rules, objectives and strategies in order to achieve this. A retrospective global examination of all the elements on which I worked clearly reveals the intentions behind my policy.

Establishing Breguet's worldwide reputation struck me as being the key objective. I was driven by great passion but this was not enough; I needed to develop a well thought-out strategy, a visionary policy and strong partnerships.

Political games were played out over the years in several acts and with several parties. I initially considered what was already in place and as these elements constituted important assets, I decided to work with them.

Firstly, Breguet was able to draw upon Chaumet's aura.

All over the world, this name was synonymous with excellence and luxury in jewellery. Chaumet's international clientele, which was both demanding and cultivated, had placed its trust in this company with its long and famous reputation.

I developed Breguet under these auspices. Paris, New York, London, Brussels, Geneva, the five Chaumet shops and particularly "Les Temporelles Chaumet" on Place Vendôme, were to be the platforms of choice for presenting Breguet – as too was my position at the head of Chaumet Jewellery in Japan.

But the game was also played out at the royal court of Morocco with his Majesty King Hassan II and the above-described relationship. Very naturally and in due course, I introduced him to Breguet with its inherent quality and elegance.

On other fronts, in Japan, Ken Takakura was a prestigious ambassador for Breguet. My meeting with the extremely famous actor took place at the French embassy in Tokyo. I gave him a Breguet watch and we had an enjoyable discussion that lasted more than three hours. This was the first of many meetings. Our friendship based on mutual esteem and respect continued to grow. We often exchanged ideas on themes that particularly interested us, such as beauty, elegance, cultural heritage, work ethics, family sentiment and traditions. Ken Takakura passed away in November 2014.

In May 2000, during an interview conducted by Ikuro Takano, editor of *Seven Seas* magazine, Ken Takakura said: "Mr Bodet is on a constant quest for beauty. And he gives

Ken Takakura and François Bodet in Tokyo (© Yoshitane Nakamoto)

a lot of thought to his work. It seems to me that I hear the nostalgic sound of the soul emanating from every watch that Mr Bodet brings into the world. In Japan as well, in the crafts world, there are sabre forgers who make us sense a certain degree of spirituality, over and above the simple manufacturing of objects. This is the same thing that we feel with Mr Bodet."

The aura surrounding Ken Takakura, the most respected of all Japanese actors, influenced Breguet's image over an entire area of Asia. I was very grateful to him for this honour.

In Japan, I was also able to count on Nathalie Itoh, my colleague, as much when I represented the House of Chaumet as when promoting Breguet and Jaquet-Droz. She was an exceptional diplomat to whom I owe a great deal!

Because traditional Europe was hard to persuade, my idea was to tackle it from the outside. Country after country, the European markets were influenced by Breguet's success in Asia, and each was in turn conquered as it opened up to Breguet's excellent technical and aesthetic qualities. Because no man is a prophet in his own land, this policy worked wonderfully.

In the nicest possible way, the cultural side of things is the stuff of dreams for the average Asian, who is able to combine it with his fascination for practical and economic aspects. Asia's craze for Breguet was bound to have an impact on Europe.

There was no question of full frontal attacks, strong-arm tactics or forcing the issue. The Breguet brand was to be gently set like a gem on the souls of refined, elegant, cultivated individuals who are ambassadors of beauty and excellence. It was about stirring desire and eliciting wonderment, about persuading from a distance before dazzling at close distance. My way of thinking and acting, with regard to this Breguet policy, never ceased to be that of a jeweller, in love with the creation upon which he remains intently focused, always with great delicacy, but with firm, determined gestures.

Taking part in exhibitions was also a strategy we used in order to escape from the relative confidentiality of stores and introduce the brand to a wider audience. Consequently, Breguet was present at the Bijorca watch and jewellery fair at the Porte de Versailles in Paris, followed by the first showing in Basel in 1983 and every subsequent year. Other highlights of Breguet's international representation included the major exhibitions held in 1986 in Chaumet's five boutiques across the world, as well as the international Antiquorum exhibition in 1991. Beauty and prestige naturally elicited wonderment and admiration.

Partnerships were a major element in my policy. Nothing is possible if one remains in isolation, but combining energies and excellence brings projects to life. Achieving a first-rate end result depends on a variety of qualities. In this respect, Tiffany and its three or four stores in the United States played an important role in my strategy.

However, I also associated Breguet with a number of private collectors (Theodor Beyer, Thomas Engels, John Asprey) and Haute Horlogerie personalities, such as André Curtit and Frédy Jeanjaquet, director of Les Ambassadeurs in Geneva. Other alliances were formed with Swiss, American and other museums.

Right from the first day that I started working on Breguet's awakening, I ensured that others talked about the brand and not just me. I activated various levers with this in mind, resulting in each individual adding to and emphasising a very positive aspect of Breguet's image. This way of doing things was more effective than promoting my own opinions.

However, the policy I wished to implement for the company also needed to apply within the company. I needed to be a visionary and to think three to five years ahead with the teams in terms of design, manufacturing and marketing. This was necessary in order to generate the requisite turnover per country and to secure their future prospects for three or more years at a time.

Our watchmakers were immediately recognised and very well accepted among manufacturers. This phenomenon enabled us to recruit other watchmakers. The quality of the team in place and the harmonious working atmosphere prevailing in the workshops was a key part of this dynamic. The Breguet watchmakers converted our suppliers to the mindset and quality of the brand, as well as favourably influencing sales agents.

Breguet's agents and retailers in each country played an important role in the policy I practised. They were cultivated people and they spread Breguet's aura through the finesse and richness of their own culture.

I used another driving factor in China, where contacts with influential men had a definite impact in the media.

A keen watchmaking enthusiast and shrewd connoisseur in this field, Pierre Aubert – by then a former President of the Swiss Confederation – gave me a lot of help at a diplomatic level. We often had friendly meetings regarding the development of the brand. He agreed to be President of the "Fondation Breguet", a fact of which I was immensely proud.

Thanks to his friendship, many Swiss embassies all over the world and particularly in Asia opened their doors to me, including the one in Beijing. I was accepted into the Forbidden City, accompanied by the minister of the city and was thus able to visit the very famous museum located in its basements and not open to the public. During these trips, I created contacts with influential people who broadcast Breguet's image in the press.

All the above-mentioned criteria were the foundations upon which Breguet's rise was founded. They were the spearheads of my policy designed to create a truly international presence for Breguet.

Fate had brought the jeweller that I was face to face with a sleeping beauty. I had cherished the goal of revealing Breguet to the world, of making its name known far and wide, of endowing it with prestige on all continents, taking it from the status of object-watch to horological treasure… This has now been accomplished and I am sometimes amazed when, for example, during an auction at Sotheby's, certain people I recognise

Historical power-reserve pocket watch
that served as initial model.

Breguet self-winding
power-reserve watch,
1982.

come up to me and say: "Mr Bodet! 1980, Breguet's 3130 self-winding power reserve!" These people have come to associate my name with Breguet and Breguet with one of its most beautiful creations.

My personal sense of satisfaction also stems from the fact that after Breguet's launch and the successes achieved from 1975 to 1987 and 1987 to 1996, the brand continued to develop magnificently under Nicolas Hayek.

I would like to pay special tribute to all the watchmakers, and all the agents as well as the early retailers, in particular Mr Kirchhofer in Interlaken, Embassy in Lucerne with Mr Koenig, not to mention the many others who subsequently contributed to Breguet's success.

Over the years, I have had the immense privilege of excellent lessons learnt from various sources. I have welcomed them with interest, as one complemented the other, enriching and adjusting my mindset to various situations. This is the kind of knowledge that no school, no book and no university could ever have given me. I have named my masters throughout this book: my parents, Jacques Gay, Georges Pellegrin, Jacques Biennenfeld, Georges Schmaus, as well as Jacques and Pierre Chaumet and André Curtit. From all of these individuals, I have received and developed a sense of discretion, perspicacity and situational analysis, as well as a flair for strategic alliances.

We should never forget those who enabled our talent to develop. My work was based on the strength and finesse of all that was passed on to me, and which helped me to build the tools and forge the various phases of my policies. My contribution was an inextinguishable passion burning deep in my heart! Breguet's renaissance depended on a combination of all these factors.

*Over the years,
I have had
the immense
privilege
of excellent lessons
learnt from
various sources*

Breguet Tourbillon
Watch, 1990

Wearing a Breguet,
Is about wearing a history,
technical quality
and hand craftsmanship
It's a truly fabulous experience!

AFTERWORD

One of the motivations for writing this book was the desire to pass on the tools used to engineer Breguet's rise.

In the present age of information technology, standardisation and a tendency to favour quantity to the detriment of quality, I wished to highlight the important role of human beings, of relationships, of harmonious teamwork and respect for different cultures. These are the kind of elements that should never be forgotten in all that is undertaken. As Ken Takakura said in the above-mentioned interview: "It is easy to have feelings for things that require care and things which take time. But people today are not educated and do not live by feeling things that are filled with emotion."

We have often discussed this exact point of a philosophy that we share. During this same interview, the chief editor of *Seven Seas*, Ikuro Takano, asked me: "Mr Bodet, could you leave a message for young Japanese people?"

I replied – and my answer is applicable to all young people: "I would like them to know that when one is 20, one cannot know everything there is to know about the world. When I was 20, I sold precious stones measuring one third of a carat and at 21 years old, stones measuring half a carat. With experience, one can learn to sell big stones. The important thing is to emphasise the role of time in the evolution of knowledge. Be it for an actor, a precious stone or a watch, everything takes time when one is aiming for perfection."

François Bodet

THE EARLY WATCHMAKERS AND EMPLOYEES – ACKNOWLEDGEMENTS

- **Daniel Roth**, 1975. Gouache sketches for new models (designer). Manufacture of perpetual calendars completely by hand. Maker of ultra-thin pivots. Management of the workshops at Le Brassus and technical offices. Contacts with all suppliers.

- **Louis Maurice Caillet**, January 1976. Still with Breguet today. Watch casing-up and hand-fitting. Construction and manufacture of prototypes for simple calendars, perpetual calendars, power reserves, openworked watches, watch and clock exteriors. Development of overall and detailed plans for the exterior and the mechanism. Ordering of mechanism parts and stock-taking (supplier relations). Installation of machines and workbenches in the workshops.

- **Jean-Louis Sautebin**, January 1977. Watch casing-up and hand-fitting. Classiques collection. Assembly and setting into function of perpetual calendars.

- **Nicole Roth**, 1977. Secretarial duties. Reception. Telephone. Invoicing. Customs documentation. Janitorial work.

- **Eugène Vidoudez**, October 1977. Head of the calendar and assembly workshop. Setting into function of calendars.

- **Marcel Depraz**, 1979. Watch casing-up and hand-fitting on Classique, ultra-thin and openworked collection.

- **Nelly Cretin**, 1979. Secretarial duties. Reception. Telephone. Invoicing. Customs documentation. Certificates for bracelets, etc.

- **Anne Fabien**,1980. Marketing assistant. Colleague. Marketing director – France.

- **Paul-André Golay**, 1981. Winding of ultra-thin movements. Piguet 70P ebauches. Adjustment of 70P and casing-up. Creation of a workshop and an excellent team for assembly of the famous 70P, in Morges.

- **Stephan Leutwiler**, 1981. Assembly and setting into function of simple and perpetual calendars. Assembly and setting into function of power reserves. Manufacture of prototypes. Islamic calendar, etc.

- **Martine Ruch**, 1986. Her passion for Breguet, her devotion and commercial skills led to her become head of the Swiss market.

- **Gilbert Rochat**, 1981. Assembly and setting into function of simple and perpetual calendars. Construction and QSE (simple off-centred date) designs in collaboration with Louis-Maurice Caillet. Assembly and setting into function of the QSE. Technical Director since 1988.

- **Denys Capt**, 1981. Head of administration. Customs formalities. Manufacturing set-up.

- **Pierre Aubert**, 1981. Cutting out of openworked clock ébauches. Filing and finishes on table clock pillars (5 glasses). Case polishing.

- **Louis Dumas**, 1981. Watchmaker. Chaumet after-sales service, Breguet and historical Breguet pieces in Paris, Place Vendôme.

- **Joseph Szuhansky**, 1985. Complications.

- **André Curtit**, 1989. Curator and my advisor on historical matters.

- **Fredy Capt**, 1985. Head of hand-fitting and casing-up. Head of Breguet building security.

- **Ding Zhixiang** (Shanghai). Advisor in China who was my translator and assistant at my seminars.

- **Albert Hausamann** (Hong Kong). One of Breguet's main agents. Highly experienced in watchmaking in Hong Kong, China, and throughout Asia.

- **Helmut Teriet** (Düsseldorf). Breguet agent.

- **Giovanni Sutti** (Milan). Breguet agent, creator of the Breguet a cultural magazine

- **Marcus Margoulis** (London). Time Products. Closely connected to the sultanates.

Published in *Begin,* a Japanese luxury watch magazine in summer 2006, the manga retraces Breguet's adventure since Chaumet.

A manga reads from right to left. We have chosen to publish the pages in the left-to-right direction so as to enable a chronological reading of the summary.

This is the story of a passion – a passion for the renaissance of Breguet – the passion of a man who brought 200 years of glorious watches back to life and who believed that watches could open up new vistas as jewelry items.

Winter 1973

The Chaumet jewellery company is located at the Place Vendôme. It was founded by Marie-Etienne Nitot in 1780 who became famous when he was appointed official jeweller to Napoleon 1st. In 1907, the boutique work-shops move to 12, Place Vendôme. François Bodet, born to a family of four generations of well-known jewellers in France, is 31 years old at the time.

After studying jewellery design, fine art and art history, he works as an expert in precious stones.

In 1972, he joins the House of Chaumet, a Parisian jeweller. He undertakes to rebuild Breguet that has been taken over by Chaumet.

The first wristwatch for men created by Chaumet is the 12, named after the number of the boutique on the Place Vendôme. Designed by Gérald Genta in his youth, the new-look rectangular case creates a sensation. Bodet dreams of launching a great watch brand.

1952. Angers in France. Bodet is ten years old. His father is a watchmaker-jeweller, his mother a pianist and artist and Bodet shows a keen interest in jewellery and the arts from an early age.

In 1963, Bodet enrols in a watchmaking school at the age of 21. His father manages the watchmaking dealership which sells Rolex in France for the first time.
Bodet obtains his certificate of professional aptitude – a qualification required to be a professional watchmaker, usually obtained by young apprentice watchmakers.

115

Paris. 1965.
Bodet studies jewellery and watchmaking with great enthusiasm at the *Ecole de Dessins de Bijoux* in Paris.
Parallel to studying watchmaking at the *Ecole de Dessins de Bijoux* in Paris, Bodet studies painting at the *Ecole du Louvre*. Bodet desperately wants to recreate some the amazing watches worn in former times.

Breguet Records
After founding the company in Paris in 1775, Breguet maintained a record of all the details of his watch production and sales. This heritage has been conserved at the Breguet Museum in Paris, and contains references to famous clients such as Marie-Antoinette and Napoleon 1st.

London. 1967.
Fascinated by jewellery, Bodet goes to study gemmology in London. Amongst other things, he works on watch repairs at the Omega workshop.

その後 ボデは宝石店ベルグリンに入社 宝石 貴金属の買い付けにフランス各地を回った

ベルグリン
ヴァンドーム広場に引けをとらない程の格式と店構えで、当時は南フランス一有名なジュエラーとして名を馳せた。マルセイユのメインストリートであるカノビエに位置していた

フランス マルセイユ ベルグリンのブティック

どうだい？ 私のデザインしたジュエリーの売れ行きは

なかなか好調ですよ

それは良かった！

お帰りなさいませ

ああ お疲れさま

最近 機械時計はクォーツに押され気味だと言うがジュエリーの需要は減らないんだな

しかし クォーツショック以後 機械式腕時計の産業は斜陽の影が差し始めていた

クォーツショック
機械式腕時計と比較して圧倒的に誤差が少なく更に大量生産によるコストダウンを実現したクォーツ腕時計は1970年代の時計市場を席巻した。これによりスイスなどの高級機械式時計ブランドは壊滅的な打撃を受け大幅に衰退した。これをクォーツショックという

時計の技術を得て 宝飾について学びセールスの技術を身に着けたボデはまさに時計界に華々しく飛び立とうとしていた

よし 次は時計だ！

Bodet joins a jewellery company called Pellegrin in Marseille and travels all over France to buy precious stones and precious metals. Pellegrin is regarded as the most famous jeweller in the South of France at that time, worthy of the boutique on Place Vendôme in every respect. Recently, people have been saying that quartz watches have been doing better than their mechanical counterparts. Bodet is convinced that watches are the future and having already studied watch and jewellery techniques, including sales, decides he is ready to take on the world of horology.

But the crisis caused by the introduction of quartz wrist-watches causes the mechanical watch industry to crash.

The quartz wristwatch is more accurate and cheaper and easier to produce in large quantities than the mechanical wristwatch that have dominated the international market since the 1970s, with the result that manufacturers of mechanical wristwatches in Switzerland and other countries are dealt a fatal blow and go into a serious decline. This becomes known as the "Quartz Crisis".

1972.
Bodet goes to work for Chaumet where he is put in charge of the watchmaking boutique. He is convinced of the importance of a company's human resources, the need to maintain client satisfaction and the fact that clients seek prestige in a watch.

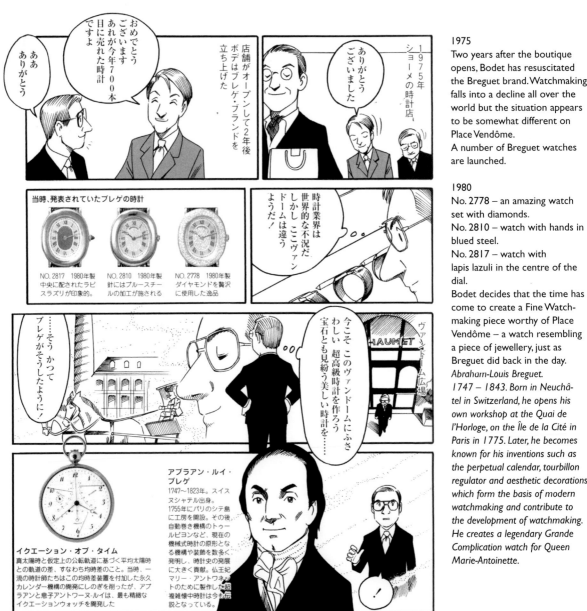

1975
Two years after the boutique opens, Bodet has resuscitated the Breguet brand. Watchmaking falls into a decline all over the world but the situation appears to be somewhat different on Place Vendôme.
A number of Breguet watches are launched.

1980
No. 2778 – an amazing watch set with diamonds.
No. 2810 – watch with hands in blued steel.
No. 2817 – watch with lapis lazuli in the centre of the dial.
Bodet decides that the time has come to create a Fine Watchmaking piece worthy of Place Vendôme – a watch resembling a piece of jewellery, just as Breguet did back in the day.
Abraham-Louis Breguet.
1747 – 1843. Born in Neuchâtel in Switzerland, he opens his own workshop at the Quai de l'Horloge, on the Île de la Cité in Paris in 1775. Later, he becomes known for his inventions such as the perpetual calendar, tourbillon regulator and aesthetic decorations which form the basis of modern watchmaking and contribute to the development of watchmaking. He creates a legendary Grande Complication watch for Queen Marie-Antoinette.

Equation of time
The discrepancy between two kinds of solar time. Watchmakers at this time sought to develop a perpetual calendar which displayed the equation. Abraham-Louis Breguet and his son Antoine-Louis succeeded in perfecting this concept with the most sophisticated mechanism in the world.

Paris
Bodet becomes involved in marketing immediately in order to achieve his dream. Mechanical watch sales are still struggling due to quartz watches. Bodet goes out looking for antique Breguet watches. He finds a number of them in an antique watch store and is told they sell well.
1818: No. 3043 – quarter-repeater cylinder hunter pocket-watch with Breguet hands and guilloche enhancing the dial.
1825: No. 2835 – watch with moon-phase and diverse, well-balanced indications. Meticulous attention to decorative detail.
1809: No. 1865 – quarter-repeater watch. Rare small seconds between 3 and 4 o'clock.
1809: No. 1176 – tourbillon watch sold to Count Potocki of St. Petersburg.
And the Tourbillon … one of Breguet's great masterpieces …

ブレゲのアンティークウォッチ

NO. 2835　1825年製
多彩な機能が文字盤にバランスよく配置された天文時計。細かな装飾が美しい。

NO. 3043　1818年製
クォーターリピーター機能を搭載。ブレゲ針やギョーシェに格調高さがあらわれる。

NO.1176　1809年製
サンクト・ペテルブルクのポトツキ伯に販売されたトゥールビヨン機構搭載の懐中時計。

NO. 1865　1809年代製
クォーターリピーター機能を搭載。4時位置にインダイヤルを配置した逸品。

121

1980
The Breguet perpetual calendar wristwatch is born. It is a complicated watch made by Daniel Roth and brilliant watchmakers circa 1978. The cabochon crown, Breguet hands, dial enhanced with guilloché décor, and perpetual calendar display are all perfectly balanced while maximising Breguet's know-how. Contrary to all expectations, the Breguet perpetual calendar is a huge success with clients on Place Vendôme. Now the mechanical watch industry has a good chance of recovery.

Bodet transfers the Breguet workshop from Paris to Switzerland. He invites two highly skilled watchmakers to join them – Louis-Maurice Caillet and Daniel Roth. L.-M. Caillet is a fantastic prototype maker who works on the revival of Breguet with Daniel Roth. Nicknamed Titi, he continues his watchmaking activities today.

After working for Jaeger-LeCoultre and Audemars Piguet, Daniel Roth reproduces exact Breguet heritage watches at Chaumet's request.

Roth and Caillet make a great contribution to the Breguet brand at the time of its revival and the meeting between the two watchmakers and Bodet is key to Breguet acquiring its great reputation.

1983. Breguet workshop. It takes them nearly three years to perfect their tourbillon wristwatch.

While researching the mean variation of rate in the vertical position, Abraham-Louis Breguet noticed that the earth's gravity is the enemy of the regularity of horological movements. The tourbillon – the mysterious device designed by him to solve the problem – was his greatest invention.

While mechanical watches stagnate, Bodet's strategic project to launch Fine Watch-making pieces succeeds. It will be the Breguet Renaissance that spearheads the mechanical watch revival.

1987. Le Brassus, Switzerland. Breguet separates from Chaumet and transfers its workshop to Le Brassus in the Vallée de Joux, known as "the holy land of fine watchmaking". Just as they are about to begin to manufacture watches completely independently, somebody breaks in and steals Breguet's movements. This leads to serious problems for the company. Bodet is determined that nobody should lose their jobs. His determination to retain these talented people strengthens the solidarity amongst the employees. In the end, nobody leaves the company.

ブレゲミュージアム

パリのヴァンドーム広場に位置しブレゲ社の伝統的な製造台帳と販売台帳をミュージアム内の金庫に厳重に保管。これらブレゲの貴重な遺産は時計界全体の重要な遺産となっている

その後店舗は修理専門工房とブレゲの歴史資料館として活用されるようになった

ヴァンドーム広場

１９８８年ブレゲ・ブランドは投資会社インベスト・コープに委譲されアトリエは再び活気を取り戻した

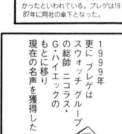

インベスト・コープ

当時、ロンドンに拠点を置く投資会社で今日のブレゲの成功はインベスト・コープの支えなしでは成し得なかったといわれている。ブレゲは1987年に同社の傘下となった。

1980年代後半に発表されたブレゲ

NO. 2765

この腕時計は、エキセントリックダイヤルが特徴的な懐中時計「モントレ・ア・タクト」ブレゲNO.4579から発想を得て製作された。カレンダーやムーンフェイズ機構を搭載する。

2003年発表のブレゲ

5207BA／12／9 V 6

「クラシック」コレクションのモデル。ブレゲの伝統ともいえる卓越した美的感覚を備える。18KYGケース。自動巻き。241万5000円

2005年発表のブレゲ

ブレゲ・トラディション

ブレゲの製作した懐中時計の意匠や機構を腕時計に再現。往年のパラシュート機構を搭載。18KYGケース。手巻き。262万5000円

１９９９年更にブレゲはスウォッチ・グループの総帥ニコラス・G・ハイエックのもとに移り現在の名声を獲得した

1988

Breguet is acquired by Investment Corp. Once again the workshop is a hive of activity. The investment company sets up its headquarters in London. The Place Vendôme Boutique serves as the after-sales service workshop and subsequently to house Breguet's historical archives.

Also located on Place Vendôme, the Breguet Museum is home to the legendary manufacturing and sales records kept under lock and key in a safe. This precious heritage also belongs to the entire watchmaking world.

No. 2765: Breguet watch launched in the second half of 1980 – characterized by the eccentric dial inspired by Breguet's No. 4759 fob watch, with calendar and moon-phase.

Breguet watch launched in 2003: part of the Classique collection, the aesthetics of this watch are peculiar to Breguet. 18-carat gold case, self-winding movement.

Breguet watch launched in 2005: Breguet Tradition - inspired by the "subscription" watches designed by Abraham-Louis Breguet, it emulates the same aesthetics and mechanism, with a *pare-chute* shock-absorbing device from earlier times.

1999
The Breguet group is acquired by Swatch Group, which is headquartered in Bienne/Biel, Switzerland. Bodet becomes an advisor to Swatch Group. He leaves this position in 2001.

2006
Omotésandou in Tokyo, Japan. In Japan too, mechanical watches are not simply in fashion, they are highly appreciated by many people.
At Baselworld this year, Breguet's new watches will enchant watch enthusiasts from all over the world. Breguet's brilliant booth particularly stands out at this fantastic fair. Without the passion devoted by Bodet who tried to revive a glorious brand through wisdom that he alone possessed 30 years ago, the booth would not exist as it is today.
But over and above this, thanks to Bodet's efforts, the renaissance of the mechanical wristwatch was made possible after the quartz crisis.
The tale of its great contribution and Breguet's glory will be told forever.

I am particularly grateful to Mrs Françoise Favre, who successfully put this path into words, for listening patiently and attentively to my account, as well as for her literary talent.

I sincerely thank Louis-Maurice Caillet, watchmaker in the Vallée de Joux, for his precious technical and historical collaboration on this book.

Thanks are also due to Mrs Eveylne Guilhaume who provided the impetus for the first edition of this book.

I also thank my wife, Marie-Laure, for her patient contribution to this publication right from the start.

I would also like to express my appreciation for the beautiful work of the three artists and writers who contributed to this book:

Photographer Mr Yoshitane Nakamoto for his great photograph of Mr Ken Takakura and me in the *Seven Seas* magazine, May 2000.

Mr Kungfu Nakano for his very realistic manga comic illustration which appeared in *Begin*, summer 2006.

Mr Yasutoshi Murakawa, author of the excellent script accompanying the *Breguet Renaissance* manga comic.

Thanks to all three of you for your kindness and for giving permission to use your work.